2012

Happ
Mum,
So much!

Maria
xxx

GW00372739

Alison Reynolds is both a loving mother and daughter. She lives in a creaking old house, on top of a hill, with her family that includes two dogs, Toby and Molly. When Alison writes, her dogs keep her company by chewing her pens and sitting as close to the heater as possible. Alison is an Australian author who has many books to her credit.

For You
Mum

Alison Reynolds

The Five Mile Press

For my mother

Jill Thelma Maurine Veitch

With love

The Five Mile Press Pty Ltd
1 Centre Road, Scoresby
Victoria 3179 Australia
www.fivemile.com.au

First published 2011

Printed and bound in Australia by McPherson's Printing Group.
Printed on paper from sustainable regrowth forests.

Cover design by Aimee Zumis
Page design by Zoë Murphy

National Library of Australia Cataloguing-in-Publication entry

Reynolds, Alison

For you, mum / Alison Reynolds.

ISBN: 9781742486529 (hbk.)

Mothers – Poetry.
Motherhood – Quotations.
Mothers – Quotations.
Motherhood – Quotations, maxims, etc.
Mothers – Anecdotes.

A828.4

Contents

Introduction ... 7

CHAPTER 1

Behind every success is a mum ... 9

CHAPTER 2

Great expectations ... 19

CHAPTER 3

Morphing into mum ... 63

CHAPTER 4

Colder than a mother-in-law's kiss ... 71

CHAPTER 5

Mothers in the house ... 89

CHAPTER 6

Remarkable mothers ... 99

CHAPTER 7

Working mums ... 107

CHAPTER 8

Motherchef ... 111

CHAPTER 9

Mummy types ... 117

CHAPTER 10

Mother and child ... 121

CHAPTER 11

Mum's the word ... 129

CHAPTER 12

Bringing up baby ... 137

CHAPTER 13

Singing the motherhood blues ... 145

CHAPTER 14

Mums of a certain age ... 157

CHAPTER 15

Loving our mothers ... 161

Introduction

Although we physically separate from our mothers at birth, we never emotionally leave them. Invisible bonds tie us to our mums for our entire life, and them to us.

A mother can be a best friend, a confidant, a mentor and a counsellor. She can be your greatest fan or your harshest critic, but you can never escape her. And for most of us, that's just how we want it.

There is a saying, 'A mother is only as happy as her unhappiest child.' Once you are a mother it's as if you've peeled a dozen layers off your skin. Sometimes rearing children is like trudging through a dank, mud-sucking swamp, then one day there's a glimmer of wonder, which bursts into pure joy.

In the following pages you will discover witty mums, tricky mums and mums who do the best they can. This book celebrates all the different stages of being a mother, from pregnancy to the grave.

For all the mothers out there, 'We love you, Mum!'

Alison Reynolds

CHAPTER 1

Behind every success is a mum

Whenever someone achieves greatness,
there's usually a mother lurking close by.
It may be a loving mum, or a pushy mum,
but most mothers are there,
smiling proudly.

IT'S ALL THANKS TO MUM

If my daughter Liza
wants to become an actress,
I'll do everything to help her.

OLIVE SCHREINER, AUTHOR — JUDY GARLAND

There was never a great man
who had not a great mother.

OLIVE SCHREINER, AUTHOR

It seems to me that my mother was the most splendid woman I ever knew ... I have met a lot of people knocking around the world since, but I have never met a more thoroughly refined woman than my mother. If I have amounted to anything, it will be due to her.

CHARLIE CHAPLIN

A MOTHER WHO WASN'T A BAT,
BUT BOUGHT ONE

The seventeen-year-old Donald Bradman played with
second-hand bats passed on by older players, until his
mother promised to buy him a brand-new bat of his
own if he made a century for Bowral, his local team.
Bradman made 300 and his mother bought a bat.
Mrs Bradman wrote in 1930 that, 'I am very proud
of Don, he is not only a good cricketer but he has
always been a good living boy.'

MOTHERS WHO GOT IT RIGHT

The boy was to build beautiful buildings.
I intend him to be an architect.

HANNAH 'ANNA' WRIGHT, MOTHER OF FRANK LLOYD WRIGHT

❧

The doctors told me that I would never walk,
but my mother told me I would,
so I believed my mother.

WILMA RUDOLPH, AMERICAN ATHLETE

MOTHERS WHO HELPED TO
CREATE THE DREAM

Fifty-four years of love and tenderness and cross-ness and devotion and unswerving loyalty. Without her I could have achieved a quarter of what I have achieved, not only in terms of success and career, but in terms of personal happiness ... She has never stood between me and my life, never tried to hold me too tightly, always let me go free ...

NOËL COWARD, PLAYWRIGHT/ACTOR

❧

[Mother was] ... a real model, not only for being a strong, intelligent woman but for proving you could reinvent yourself with enough willpower and personal strength. [She told me]... memorably as I was growing up, 'I am not going to teach you how to cook or how to do housework because if I do you will become some man's domestic servant.'

KATE GRENVILLE, AUTHOR

❧

HANDS-ON MUMS

A teacher told Thomas Edison's mother that Thomas couldn't learn, was 'addled', and asked too many questions. Nancy Edison withdrew her son from school and homeschooled him, encouraging Thomas to learn things for himself. When Thomas was nine, Nancy Edison gave him an elementary science book. It explained how to do chemistry experiments at home.

Edison did every experiment in the book.

-•-

Newly arrived Welsh immigrant Moira Gillard, mother of Australian Prime Minister Julia Gillard, was determined to provide her children with a decent education and a chance at a better life. Every night when she returned home from work, Moira taught the four-year-old Julia and her sister Alison to read and write. Both Julia and Alison could read by the time they attended kindergarten.

SOME MOTHERS TRY TO BE HELPFUL WITH THE CAREER BUT ...

Spin bowler Shane Warne was banned from playing cricket for twelve months after he tested positive to a diuretic drug. Warne claimed his mother gave him a tablet to help him look a bit trimmer for the cameras when he announced his retirement from one-day cricket.

MUMS THAT EXPECT, AND KIDS THAT DELIVER

I think it's something you're born with. No-one in our family [is] business minded or has ever run a business. Ruslan was the first to have a desire to control his own financial freedom and prosperity. All I did was ensure he went to school, studied hard – and came top of his class.

IRENE KOGAN, MOTHER OF SUCCESSFUL YOUNG AUSTRALIAN ENTREPRENEUR, RUSLAN KOGAN

❧

Oh, I think mum seemed to have had some view about it [being Australian prime minister] you know when I was born, I don't know she said there was something special but that's a bit embarrassing to talk about.

BOB HAWKE, EX-AUSTRALIAN PRIME MINISTER

My mum [Anca] had a saying that, 'Can't is dead'. She would never let me come to her and say, 'I can't do this.'

BRUNO SCHIAVI, YOUNG AUSTRALIAN ENTREPRENEUR

The story I tell that sums up my mother is when I got ninety-eight per cent for a music exam and she said, 'What a pity about the two other marks.' It's become a saying in my family, if I ever get a little bit [she mimes looking pleased with herself] they say, 'Pity about the other two marks.'

QUENTIN BRYCE, AUSTRALIAN GOVERNOR-GENERAL

HARD-TO-CONVINCE MUMS

My mother really wanted me to pass well at the university and have a degree so that I could get a job. That's it. She would call it 'qualifications'. What really worried her was that I had no qualifications and this writing lark that I was doing would never really pay properly and I wouldn't be able to build a house for my family, the way she had, which she did all by herself. This went on for several decades and she never quite believed what I was doing – she'd watch me on television and she was still worrying about the qualifications.

Then finally, a few years ago, the Sydney University very kindly gave me an honorary doctorate, a doctor in letters ... My mother was there. I'd got her – they brought her down from the nursing home, she's in a wheelchair and she was sitting there at the back of the hall and I gave the address. After that I walked towards her and there could almost have been a brass band playing selections from *Aida*, you know, as I marched towards her. I could see this look on her face and I knew what that look was. She was thinking, 'At last he's got his qualifications.'

CLIVE JAMES, AUTHOR

MUMS WHO MAY HAVE GOT IT WRONG

The young Frank Sinatra idolised Bing Crosby and not only smoked a pipe like Bing, but he also wore a white yachting cap. His mother Dolly got fed up. She wanted Frank to be a doctor or civil engineer. When she saw Crosby's picture on Frank's bedroom wall, she threw a shoe at her son and called him a bum.

❧

My mother has always
been unhappy with what I do.
She would rather I did something nicer,
like be a bricklayer.

MICK JAGGER

❧

My mother said to me,
'If you become a soldier you'll be a general;
if you become a monk you'll end up as the Pope.'
Instead, I became a painter
and wound up as Picasso.

PABLO PICASSO

❧

That guitar is okay

but you'll never make a living with it.

❧

I wiggle my shoulders. I shake my legs.

I walk up and down the stage. I hop around

on one foot. But I never bump and grind.

I'd never do anything vulgar before an audience.

My mother would never allow it.

ELVIS PRESLEY

❧

Albert Einstein's mother thought he was deformed as he had such a big, misshapen head when he was born. He seldom spoke as a child, and if he did it was extremely slowly, so his mother and father believed he was mentally challenged. Finally, he broke his usual silence at the supper table one night to say normally, 'The soup is too hot'. His relieved parents asked why he had never said a word before. Albert replied, 'Because up to now everything was in order.'

❧

CHAPTER 2

Great Expectations

Once a woman is pregnant,
her life is never the same.

MAKING THE CHOICE

Making the decision to have a child is momentous.
It is to decide forever to have your heart go
walking around outside your body.

ELIZABETH STONE, AUTHOR

❧

Life is tough enough
without having someone kick you
from the inside.

RITA RUDNER, COMEDIAN

❧

Pregnancy seemed like
a tremendous abdication of control.
Something growing inside you
which would eventually usurp your life.

ERICA JONG, AUTHOR

❧

If men were equally at risk from this condition – if they knew their bellies might swell as if they were suffering from end-stage cirrhosis, that they would have to go nearly a year without a stiff drink, a cigarette, or even an aspirin, that they would be subject to fainting spells and unable to fight their way onto commuter trains – then I am sure that pregnancy would be classified as a sexually transmitted disease and abortions would be no more controversial than emergency appendectomies.

BARBARA EHRENREICH, AUTHOR

GETTING PREGNANT

Familiarity breeds contempt – and children.

MARK TWAIN, AUTHOR

It is now quite lawful for a Catholic woman
to avoid pregnancy by a resort to mathematics,
though she is still forbidden to resort to
physics and chemistry.

HL MENCHEN, JOURNALIST

Being pregnant is an occupational hazard
of being a wife.

QUEEN VICTORIA

❧

If men could get pregnant,
abortion would be a sacrament.

ROSE F KENNEDY, MOTHER OF PRESIDENT JOHN F KENNEDY

❧

It takes TWO to get one into trouble.

MAE WEST, ACTRESS

TELLING THE NEWS

I have come, Sire,
to complain of one of your subjects who has
been so audacious as to kick me in the belly.

MARIE ANTOINETTE, TELLING LOUIS XVI OF FRANCE
THAT SHE WAS PREGNANT WITH HIS CHILD

❧

Come on Joanie, he said. *Spit it out*, and I took a breath and run at the words: *It is like this Duncan, I am with child.* I almost laughed to hear what kind of quaint antique words I had chosen to break the news, so Duncan stared at a face twisted and writhing with mixed passions of amusement and dismay, and I watched him wonder if I was making a joke in poor taste, or what was happening. I tried to be clearer: *I am pregnant, Duncan,* I said bluntly, and the cold words sobered me and there was all at once, nothing to laugh at.

Kate Grenville, Joan Makes History

❧

'I'm in pig, what do you think of that?'

'A most hideous expression, Linda dear,' said Aunt
Emily, 'but I suppose we must congratulate you.'

'I suppose so,' said Linda. She sank into a chair with an
enormous sigh. 'I feel awfully ill, I must say.'

'But think how much good it will do you in the long
run,' said Davey, enviously, 'such a wonderful clearout.'

'I see just what you mean,' said Linda.

Nancy Mitford, Pursuit of Love

THE MOTHER OF URGES

I was desperate for a baby and I have the medical bills to prove it … I still have pregnancy dreams, waiting with vast joy and confidence for something that will never happen.

GERMAINE GREER, AUTHOR

❧

It would seem that something which means poverty, disorder and violence every single day should be avoided entirely, but the desire to beget children is a natural urge.

PHYLLIS DILLER, COMEDIAN

❧

I was twenty-seven, I think. I had that overwhelming, 'Oh, must have a baby!' Just couldn't bear not being pregnant. Just sort of came over me. And so I was very happy when I got pregnant, and Bridgie was born on a full moon in that little village in a little house with a little Indian midwife, and it was all very easy and beautiful and ideal, and she was gorgeous and it was lovely.

GABRIELLE CAREY, AUTHOR

❧

Having a child is surely
the most beautifully irrational act
that two people in love can commit.

Bill Cosby, humorist

It's always been very clear to me that I was going to be a mother and that my purpose in life was to give life. It's always been a thousand per cent clear in my head. It was just when. This came as a perfect surprise, and the father of my child and I are just ecstatic. It seems perfectly normal.

Interviewer: So, it wasn't planned?

You know, I could go into the details of my contraception – which I don't use. But I don't think it would be particularly interesting. Or maybe it would be far too interesting?

Elle Macpherson

FERTILITY WATERS

Nicole Kidman believes outback 'fertility waters'
near Kununurra may have contributed to her
unexpected pregnancy. When she and six of her
co-workers conceived during the production of the
film *Australia*, Kidman claimed, 'There is something
up there in the Kununurra water because we all went
swimming in the waterfalls, so we can call it the
fertility waters now.'

THE SEX OF THE BABY

I met a mother who had four girls and decided to have
one last go for a boy. Her husband was a real man's
man, so she thought he should have a boy. She had
twin girls. Maybe she should have looked at what
she ate.

MAYBE BABY BOY FOOD

These foods are said to promote the conception of boys, but this is not guaranteed.

- Bananas
- Figs
- Nuts
- Watermelon
- Baked potatoes with skins
- Coffee – this supposedly makes Y-chromosome carrying sperm swim faster
- Apricots
- Raisins
- Bran cereal
- Spinach

MAYBE BABY GIRL FOOD

These foods are said to promote the conception of girls, but this is not guaranteed.

- Fish
- Eggs
- Cranberries
- Milk
- Yoghurt
- Corn
- Meat
- Plums
- Cheese
- Leafy green vegetables

Tell your partner to have a hot bath (as opposed to a cold shower). The increase in body temperature will help the female sperm (X-chromosome carrying sperm) since they are more resistant to heat than the male kind.

WHAT ARE LITTLE BOYS MADE OF?

What are little boys made of?
Snips and snails, and puppy dogs tails
That's what little boys are made of!
What are little girls made of?
Sugar and spice and all things nice
That's what little girls are made of!

GUESSING THE SEX

My mother, who was of a scientific bent, could sex kittens by the careful use of a needle hanging from a thread. She dangled the needle above the kitten's head and if the needle spun in circles the kitten was pronounced a boy. If the needle swung back and forth, then the kitten was a girl. She was infallible until the day we received the phone call, 'Timmy's just had kittens.'

I don't want to know
if it's a boy or a girl.
I feel like it's one of
the last great mysteries of life.

Minnie Driver, actress

❧

It's not about planning a nursery, it's more about I just want to know. I want to be able to relate in that way. That's what works for me, but I totally believe in whatever works for the individual … I thought about waiting and I just don't think that's really my personality.

Amy Adams, actress

FUN, BUT OFTEN HIGHLY INACCURATE, WAYS TO GUESS THE SEX

It's a boy if:
- You didn't experience morning sickness in early pregnancy
- Your baby's heart rate is less than 140 beats per minute
- You are carrying the extra weight out front
- Your belly looks like a basketball
- Your areolas have darkened considerably
- You are carrying low
- You are craving salty or sour foods
- You are craving protein – meats and cheese
- Your feet are colder than they were before pregnancy
- The hair on your legs has grown faster during pregnancy
- Your hands are very dry
- Your pillow faces north when you sleep
- Dad-to-be is gaining weight, right along with you
- Pregnancy has you looking better than ever
- Your urine is bright yellow in colour
- Your nose is spreading
- You hang your wedding ring over your belly and it moves in circles
- You are having headaches
- You add your age at the time of conception and the number for the month you conceived and the sum is an even number

It's a girl if:

- You had morning sickness early in pregnancy
- Your baby's heart rate is at least 140 beats per minute
- You are carrying the weight on your hips and rear
- Your left breast is larger than your right breast
- Your hair develops red highlights
- You are carrying high
- Your belly looks like a watermelon
- You are craving sweets
- You are craving fruit
- You are craving orange juice
- You don't look quite as good as normal during pregnancy
- You are moodier than usual during pregnancy
- Your face breaks out more than usual
- You refuse to eat the heel of a loaf of bread
- Your breasts have really blossomed!
- Your pillow faces south when you sleep
- Your urine is a dull yellow colour
- You hang your wedding ring over your belly and it moves from side to side
- You add your age at the time of conception and the number for the month you conceived and the sum is an odd number

CHANGING SHAPE

You should never say anything to a woman
that even remotely suggests that you think she's
pregnant unless you can see an actual baby
emerging from her at that moment.

DAVE BARRY, HUMORIST

❧

Do not breed.
Nothing gives less pleasure than childbearing.
Pregnancies are damaging to health, spoil the
figure, wither the charms, and it's the cloud of
uncertainty for ever hanging over these events
that darkens a husband's mood.

MARQUIS DE SADE, FRENCH ARISTOCRAT

❧

The breasts go first
and then the waist and then the butt.
Nobody ever tells you that
you get a butt when you're pregnant.

ELLE MACPHERSON

❧

Think of stretch marks
as pregnancy service stripes.

Joyce Armor, poet

❧

Everything grows rounder and wider and weirder,
and I sit here in the middle of it all and wonder
who in the world you will turn out to be.

Carrie Fisher, actress

❧

I positively think that ladies who are
always enceinte quite disgusting; it is more like a
rabbit or a guinea pig than anything else and really
it is not very nice.

Queen Victoria

❧

The only time a woman wishes she was a year
older is when she is expecting a baby.

Mary Marsh, writer

❧

If pregnancy were a book
they would cut the last two chapters.

Nora Ephron, *Heartburn*

CELEBRATING THE CHANGES

Already the baby was becoming a person. Roie's body was still slim, but her breasts were full and aching. She hugged the soreness to herself as though it were a blessing and a privilege. The rich autumn was past; Lick Jimmy changed the yellow chrysanthemums in his window for purple everlastings and the cold winds came from the interior of the continent as bitterly as from a fireless hearth. Roie was always warm; an inward fire made her body glow. She felt a rich and drowsy contentment, like a wheatfield, heavy and burdened with its won harvest. Often she placed a hand on her abdomen and felt her baby quivering. It was so alive; it jumped when a loud noise occurred, as though it heard. Charlie and she loved to lie in bed, feeling the baby between them, moving a tiny foot or hand, perhaps turning its head a little in its cramped and sheltered haven. There was a precious secret feeling about their love of the baby's little movements, so helpless, so pathetic.

RUTH PARK, *THE HARP IN THE SOUTH*

I don't think I ever felt beautiful until I was
pregnant and when I gave birth to my children.
(I had terrible acne when I was a teenager and
I was very tall, so tall I couldn't see myself
in my mother's long mirror.)

VANESSA REDGRAVE, ACTRESS

❧

They're not very big, my boobs,
so they just became normal size.
I loved it! I felt very Woman.
When you've had a slightly androgynous body
your whole life, having breasts is a nice feeling!

NICOLE KIDMAN, ACTRESS

❧

I love being pregnant. You can do whatever you
want. You don't feel guilty, because I used to feel
guilty about having a day off. And, you know,
something really strange happened to me. Before
my pregnancies, I was someone who had to watch
their weight.

CLAUDIA SCHIFFER, MODEL

PREGNANCY KEEPSAKES

The ultrasound

Most parents cherish the often amorphous blob on the ultrasound as their baby's first photo. They place it in a photo frame, show it to family, friends and the man or woman walking down the street. You can also have the ultrasound copied onto canvas with archival ink of your colour choices, and you'll have a remembrance that lasts through the generations.

Others choose to film the actual ultrasound directly off the monitor as it's under way. Then you can upload the film to your website or YouTube and watch it with friends and family. This way everyone gets to hear the doctor explain what they're seeing, and your expression and questions are audible too.

Try a belly cast

A belly cast for pregnancy is a mould or series of moulds of a pregnant female belly and/or, breasts, arms, hands, feet and thighs, made out of plaster to commemorate the event with a lasting keepsake in 3D form that can be displayed on a wall, or show-cased on a table or a shelf instead of the flat 2D form found in photographs.

The best time to make a belly cast is between seven and nine months when the tummy is biggest. DIY kits are available and the mother is encouraged to decorate it to make it meaningful for her.

The belly casts are very popular with fathers. Some men find that belly masking allows them to bond more with their unborn child, and feel part of the pregnancy experience.

Home pregnancy test kits

According to a survey by a manufacturer of home pregnancy test kits, many expectant women are unwilling to part with the urine stick that marked the moment they knew they were a mum-to-be. This clever manufacturer offers a special container for storage of the used pregnancy kit, which is nicer for everyone than a urine-stained stick being displayed on the mantelpiece with other pregnancy keepsakes.

ANTICIPATION

I begin to love this creature,

and to anticipate her birth

as a fresh twist to a knot,

which I do not wish to untie.

MARY WOLLSTONECRAFT,
EIGHTEENTH CENTURY RADICAL

GIVING BIRTH

Heaven grant
that the burden you carry
may have as easy an exit
as it had an entrance.

ERASMUS (1465–1536),
PRAYER FOR A PREGNANT WOMAN

My mother groaned, my father wept, into the
    dangerous world I leapt,
helpless, naked, piping loud, like a fiend hid in
    a cloud.

WILLIAM BLAKE, POET

-❧-

Telegram to a friend who had just become a mother
after a prolonged pregnancy:

Good work, Mary, we all knew you had it in you.

DOROTHY PARKER, HUMORIST

-❧-

Although present on the occasion [his own birth], I have
no clear recollection of the events leading up to it.

WINSTON CHURCHILL, EX BRITISH PRIME MINISTER

-❧-

I think my life began
with waking up and
loving my mother's face.

GEORGE ELIOT, *DANIEL DERONDA*

Priss Hartshorn Crockett was nursing her baby. That was the big news. 'I never expected a breastfed grandson,' said Priss's mother, laughing and accepting a martini from her son-in-law, Dr Sloan Crockett, the budding paediatric- ian. It was the cocktail hour in Priss's room at New York Hospital – terribly gay. Over the weekend Sloan stopped in every afternoon and shook up martinis for visitors. He had done his residency at the hospital, so that he could get ice from the diet kitchen and generally break the rules.

'You never expected a g-*grandson*,' pointed out Priss with her silent nervous stammer from the bed. She was wearing a pale-blue jacket, and her thin ashy hair was set in waves; the student nurse had done it for her that morning. On her lips, which were dry, was a new shade of lipstick by Tussy; her doctor had ordered her to put on lipstick and powder right in the middle of labour; he and Sloan thought it was important for a maternity patient to keep herself up to the mark. Priss, whose personality was confessed to be rather colourless, looked unreal to herself sitting up in bed all bedecked and bedizened – like one of those New York children in furs and trailing satins and their mothers' slippers to beg at Halloween. 'Little Ella Cinders' Sloan called her, after that funny in the paper. She would have been more comfortable in the short cotton hospital night-shirt that tied in back, but the floor nurses every morning made her struggle into a satin-and-lace 'nightie' from her trousseau. Doctor's orders they said.

MARY MCCARTHY, *THE GROUP*

HARD LABOUR

It was only after I gave birth that I learned that labour was a competitive business. At mothers' groups, the mums love to share horror birth stories. One day I heard how one woman laboured for days, which another woman countered with the news that her labour was too short and too much of a shock for her body. I come from the stance that any labour is a shock to one's body.

Sit! Walk! Stand! Squat!

Get active – give birth.

FROM A T-SHIRT

❧

I had 'drugs now' written on my abdomen,

in case I lost the power of speech.

JEAN KITTSON, COMEDIAN/WRITER

❧

Offer hugs, not drugs.

ADINA LEBOWITZ, CHILD ADVOCATE

❧

Giving birth is stone age. It's prehistoric what happens to a woman in labour. During labour, if you ever had any doubt about the gender of God, then you realise that God is a bloke! Natural childbirth is a case of stiff upper labia.

KATHY LETTE, AUTHOR

❧

It was a wild night in the year of Federation that the birth took place. Horses kicked down their stables. Pigs flew, figs grew thorns. The infant mewled and stared and the doctor assured the mother that a caul was a lucky sign. *A girl?* the father exclaimed, outside in the waiting room, tiled as if for horrible emergencies. This was a contingency he was not prepared for, but he rallied within a day and announced, *Lilian*. She will be called *Lilian Una*.

Later, her mother lay on her white bed at home, her palms turned up, staring at the moulding of the ceiling with the expression of surprise she wore for the next twenty years. *You didn't tell me it would hurt*, she whispered to her friends as they patted the crocheted bed jacket, and she was already beginning to suffer her long overlapping series of indispositions. The friends picked up the baby from its crib beside the bed and placed it in the mother's arms. *A lovely picture*, they agreed, and left.

KATE GRENVILLE, *LILIAN'S STORY*

You are a midwife, assisting at someone else's birth. Do good without show or fuss. Facilitate what is happening rather than what you think ought to be happening. If you must take the lead, lead so that the mother is helped, yet still free and in charge. When the baby is born, the mother will rightly say: 'We did it ourselves!'

FROM *THE TAO TE CHING*, 300 B.C.

❧

I enjoyed giving birth to my second son in a birth pool. My birthing room was warm and candlelit and I was lovingly supported by my birthing team. This made me feel emotionally safe as I birthed my baby gently.

Elle Macpherson

❧

People are giving birth under water now. They say it's less traumatic for the baby because it's in water. But certainly more traumatic for the other people in the pool.

Elayne Boosler, comedian

❧

I am not interested in being Wonder Woman
in the delivery room. Give me drugs.

MADONNA

❧

I'm so lucky I'm so tall, so I carried small and also, I have to say, I had a birth that I was blessed with, a labour that was very good and a baby that was very good to me in that regard. They say that [an easy labour] is genetic, so I'm grateful for that because it was beautiful and Keith was my rock through it all. To be given this again is a beautiful thing. To have raised Bella and Connor since I was twenty-five and now to be able to do it again at forty-one … wow!

NICOLE KIDMAN, ACTRESS

❧

I was caesarean born. You can't really tell,
although whenever I leave a house,
I go out through the window.

STEVEN WRIGHT

Aunt Sadie, who had only just finished having her seven children, when appealed to [about pain of childbirth], was not very reassuring.

'Yes,' she said, vaguely. 'It is the worst pain in the world. But the funny thing is, you always forget in between what it's like. Each time, when it began, I felt like saying, "Oh, now I can remember, stop it, stop it." And, of course, by then it was nine months too late to stop it.'

NANCY MITFORD, *PURSUIT OF LOVE*

❧

If nature had arranged that husbands and wives
should have children alternatively,
there would never be more than three in a family.

LAWRENCE HOUSMAN, ILLUSTRATOR/AUTHOR

❧

Giving birth is like taking your lower lip
and forcing it over your head.

CAROL BURNETT, COMEDIAN

❧

Birth is very challenging in the best possible way. Every fibre of your being is alive. It's like you are conducting electricity; literally creating something. I would like to give birth every year if I could, just for the experience.

THANDIE NEWTON, ACTRESS

❧

[Childbirth] Like an orange being stuffed up your nostril.

LADY REDESDALE, ARISTOCRAT

❧

I want to have children, but my friends scare me. One of my friends told me she was in labour for thirty-six hours. I don't even want to do anything that feels good for thirty-six hours.

RITA RUDNER, COMEDIAN

❧

My sister-in-law gave birth to her first child eight years before we had children. Her birth was fast and easy. She told me the story with great enthusiasm. She had no pain relief and pushed the baby out on all fours. She smiled as she said, 'It was the best orgasm of my life!' I smiled back, but I had no idea what she was talking about.

SARAH JAMES, *MIDWIFE WISDOM, MOTHER LOVE*

MATERNITY HOSPITALS

Look, it's the maternal Nullarbor. Nothing but mothers and babies, babies and mothers as far as the eye can see. Eighteen mothers and eighteen newborn babies all rooming in together. Now, I learnt something from that experience. Oh, my God, I did! I learnt that anybody who says they sleep like a baby has never had one. But look, there were highlights to my stay in that ward. One of the highlights was the fact that they put those of us who'd had caesareans at the Melbourne end of the ward and they put the one and only toilet at the Perth end of the ward. Isn't that thoughtful? Of course, you've got to go to the toilet, so you begin the long, slow haul, doing the CCC – the caesarean crouch crawl. I don't know whether you're familiar with it. It goes a little like this. You're shaking at the time and you're holding your breasts up because they've swollen up like bowling balls. And they weigh the same as a bowling ball. Whoops! Dropped one! Caught it. And you're off to the toilet and you want to cough.

DENISE SCOTT, COMEDIAN/AUTHOR

MIAOW

In one Taiwan maternity hospital, the newborns are welcomed by Hello Kitty, the popular cartoon character. Nurses dress in pink uniforms with cat-themed aprons and the cot linen, room décor and pink and blue receiving blankets are all adorned with images of the well-known white mouthless kitty. The director believes that the Hello Kitty motif will ease the pain and fear associated with childbirth and being admitted into hospital.

❧

I remember leaving the hospital – thinking, 'Wait, are they going to let me just walk off with him? I don't know beans about babies! I don't have a licence to do this.' [We're] just amateurs.

ANNE TYLER, AUTHOR

DESIGNER MATERNITY HOSPITAL GOWNS

If you don't want to wear the generic 'one size fits no-one' hospital gown, there's always a designer hospital gown. These usually have snaps all the way down the back for full coverage (although one wonders how comfy that would be to lie on), and snaps down the sleeves to enable easy access and privacy for breastfeeding. Some even have a low-cut back for easy insertion of an epidural.

A HOSPITAL TOO FAR

Many mothers give birth in hospitals, some in homes and some in less salubrious surroundings.

- A British barmaid woke up with stabbing pains. Thirty minutes later she gave birth – in her toilet. She had no idea she was pregnant – her periods had continued as usual and there was no sign of a 'bump'. Suddenly, the woman experienced an overwhelming urge to push and she rushed to the toilet. A baby girl splashed down into the toilet bowl. Both mother and baby were well.

- A Scottish woman gave birth on a lifeboat. She and her midwife thought she had time to make it to the mainland, and initially the vibrations of the boat did seem to soothe both mother and baby. However, when the lifeboat reached the harbour the engine slowed, she had a massive contraction and her waters broke. She put her feet up on a chair opposite and three minutes later she walked with her baby from the lifeboat to an ambulance. Her Australian partner remained very chilled out during the whole experience.

- Katherine Allen didn't have time to get her pants off when her baby arrived. She gave birth to her 3.7 kilogram daughter down the leg of her grey tracksuit pants when standing at the bottom of the staircase in her house. She had been told that her contractions were too far apart to go to the hospital.

- One English woman had her baby in the local post office. Her waters broke while she waited in the queue and her baby arrived two minutes later. The capable postmistress nursed the baby until the ambulance came, taking the opportunity to weigh the newborn on the post office scale.

- A woman in Mozambique gave birth in a tree, where she sheltered from floodwaters. A rescue helicopter arrived just in time to cut the umbilical cord.

EARTHQUAKE SHAKES INDUCE LABOUR

A record number of babies were born in Christchurch Women's Hospital in the twenty-four hours after the quake that rocked New Zealand in 2010. One mother claimed the shock of the 7.4 magnitude earthquake was enough to jolt mothers into labour.

YOUNGEST MOTHER

Lina Medina was just under five years and eight months, when she delivered a 2.7 kilogram son by caesarean section. Her parents feared their daughter had a huge abdominal tumour, and when shamans in their remote village in Peru's Andes failed to discover a cure, her father carried her to a hospital. The doctors suspected a tumour, but soon discovered she was eight months pregnant. Lina Medina was diagnosed with precocious puberty: her first period occurred at eight months of age; she had prominent breast development by the age of four; and by the age of five her figure displayed pelvic widening and advanced bone maturation.

The father of the child was never identified.

OLDEST MOTHER

In 2008, seventy-year-old Omkari Panwar gave birth to twins, a boy and a girl, by emergency caesarean section in India. The babies weighed 907 grams each. Omkari became pregnant through IVF treatment, which she and her husband pursued in order to produce a male heir. Omkari has two adult daughters and five grand-children. When told she'd possibly broken the record for the world's oldest mother, Omkari stated, 'If I am the world's oldest mother it means nothing to me. I just want to see my new babies and care for them while I am still able.'

❧

Having a baby is a really great leveller as no-one gets any sleep. Because if you're sixteen or forty, you feel like you're forty.

JEAN KITTSON, COMEDIAN/PERFORMER/WRITER

❧

The media image of the older mother is a Teflon-coated apprentice-style bitch who wants it all on her own terms, and who would like to buy a baby like a Marc Jacobs handbag and then strap it into her Chelsea tractor and whoosh off to Harvey Nicks. In my experience, the women who try for babies late, and who go through the gruelling IVF hoops, are those who realise that their lives will probably feel incomplete if they don't at least try to have a baby.

CORINNE SWEET, WRITER/PSYCHOLOGIST

OLDEST MOTHER TO CONCEIVE NATURALLY

Dawn Brooks became the world's oldest mother to conceive without any fertility treatment, when she gave birth to a healthy boy at the age of fifty-nine. The pregnancy was a total surprise to Dawn who initially feared that the aches, cravings and feelings of exhaustion were signs of a serious illness. Tests revealed she was sixteen weeks pregnant.

She had two grown-up children from a previous marriage, and said: 'We never dreamed there would be an addition to the family but I'll never forget the feeling of looking into my baby boy's blue eyes after giving birth. There were no regrets then or since … [but] I get upset when I think that I might not watch him get married, see his children.'

Initially, Dawn was embarrassed by the pregnancy, but her husband Ray Brooks was thrilled. When they announced their news to family and friends, Ray was greeted with a round of applause.

OLDEST FIRST-TIME MOTHER

Rajo Devi Lohan gave birth to her first child, Naveen, at the age of seventy in Alewa, India. For years Rajo Devi and Baba Ram, her seventy-two-year-old husband, had endured village gossip and avoided neighbours at local weddings and festivals. The pressure to preserve their family's honour, part of India's village code, was so great that friends and family urged the couple to separate. 'Everyone kept telling Baba to leave me, to get someone who could have children,' says Rajo Devi.

After fifteen years of trying and failing to have a family, Baba married Omni, Rajo Devi's sister. She, too, was unable to have children, and the three of them were resigned to a childless existence until a neighbour told them about the new 'medicine'. Indian doctors do not need to take into account a mother's age, only her physique. Rajo Devi became pregnant with IVF.

'We have waited for more than forty years for this child,' she says, stroking Naveen's cheek. 'It was God's gift to us that she arrived.' She also says that she plans to breastfeed her 'for at least three years'.

The Lohans want to try for more children. Next they are hoping for a boy, to bring a dowry through marriage and retain the family name.

PROLIFIC MOTHERS

A woman came to ask the doctor if a woman
should have children after thirty-five. I said that
thirty-five children is enough for any woman.

GRACIE ALLEN, ENTERTAINER

The world's most prolific mother is known only as 'the
wife of Feodor Vassilyev', a peasant in Shuya, Russia.
She gave birth to at least sixty-nine children, including
sixteen pairs of twins, seven sets of triplets and four
sets of quadruplets in the eighteenth century.

THERE WAS AN OLD WOMAN
WHO LIVED IN A SHOE

There was an old woman who lived in a shoe.

She had so many children, she didn't know what to do.

She gave them some broth without any bread;

And whipped them all soundly and put them to bed.

ANONYMOUS

There are several versions of the origins of this nursery rhyme. Some claim the old woman was Queen Caroline, wife of King George II, who had eight children. Others claim the old woman refers to King George himself, who began the men's fashion for wearing white powdered wigs and was referred to as the 'old woman'. The children were the members of parliament and the bed was the Houses of Parliament. The English parliament still uses the term 'whip' to describe a member of parliament who is tasked to ensure that all members 'toe the party line'.

Another version is that it is based on Margery Buttwhistle, a known village drunk and prostitute. She is believed to have had in excess of twenty illegitimate children. Her children formed the notorious 'Shoe Gang' which specifically targeted the footwear of wealthy aristocrats. Mrs Buttwhistle would barter the shoes in exchange for mead, and would seldom leave the local inn at night. She would collapse drunk in the cellar with only the shoes for company.

BREASTFEEDING

The babe at first feeds upon the mother's bosom,
but is always on her heart.

HENRY WARD BEECHER, CLERGYMAN

❧

People say, 'You're still breastfeeding, that's so generous.'
Generous, no! It gives me boobs and it takes my thighs
away! It's sort of like natural liposuction. I'd carry on
breastfeeding for the rest of my life if I could.

HELENA BONHAM CARTER, ACTRESS

❧

There are three reasons for breastfeeding:
the milk is always at the right temperature;
it comes in attractive containers;
and the cat can't get it.

IRENA CHALMERS, FOOD WRITER

Mrs. Hartshorn glanced at her daughter ᵕ
'Just fancy little Priss being the first of your set to uᵕ
so flat there she's never had to wear a brassière. But Sloaᵕ
it's not the size that counts. I do hope he's right. The miracle of
the loaves and fishes, I call it. All the other babies in the nursery
are on bottles. The nurses prefer it that way. I'm inclined to agree
with them. Doctors are all theory. Nurses see the facts.' She
swallowed her martini in a single draft, like medicine; this was
the style among advanced society women of her age. She wiped
her lips and refused a 'dividend' from the silver shaker. 'Which
way progress, Polly?' she demanded, in a slightly louder voice,
shaking her white bobbed locks. 'The bottle was the war cry
of my generation. Linda was bottle-fed. And you can't imagine
the difference. For us, the bottle spelled the end of colic, and
the frantic husband walking the baby all night. We swore by the
bottle, we of the avant-garde. My mother-in-law was horripilated.
And now, I confess, Polly, I'm horripilated myself.'

'Medicine seems to be all cycles,' continued Mrs. Hartshorn.
'That's the bone I pick with Sloan. Like what's-his-name's new
theory of history. First we nursed our babies; then science told
us not to. Now it tells us we were right in the first place. Or were
we wrong then but would be right now? Reminds me of relativity,
if I understand Mr Einstein.'

MARY MCCARTHY, THE GROUP

my baby boy
so plump on milk
and love

MARY HIND, POET

KEEPING IT UNDERCOVER

When an actress takes off her clothes onscreen but a nursing mother is told to leave, what message do we send about the roles of women? In some ways we're as committed to the old madonna–whore dichotomy as ever. And the madonna stays home, feeding the baby behind the blinds, a vestige of those days when for a lady to venture out was a flagrant act of public exposure.

ANNA QUINDLAN, AUTHOR

BREASTFEEDING COVERS

These are being promoted as a convenient and discreet breast-feeding alternative. The garments are designed to cover mum – not – baby while breastfeeding, so both the baby and mum feel confident and comfortable. Some of them must also be used by mums with nerves of steel. Could you calmly follow all these instructions while you had a bellowing hungry baby on your knee?

1. When ready to nurse, simply remove the Cover from its purse and slip over your head just like you would a poncho.

2. Pull the back panels around to cover your sides, tucking them into your waistband if it makes you feel more comfortable.

3. Adjust your shirt/dress and bra in preparation for feeding.

4. To completely cover your sides, overlap the front of your Cover at the sides with the back section, which should already be tucked into place.

5. When ready to feed, position baby comfortably and lift the top layer of your Cover to reveal your breast to baby. The top layer can be draped over baby gently, just as a shirt or wrap would be. Try this step a few different ways to determine what is most comfortable for you.

6. Once baby is finished nursing, simply lower the top layer of your Cover and re-adjust your bra and shirt/dress underneath.

7. Use your Cover as protection for your clothes when burping baby ... Why not, it's machine washable after all!

8. Finally, slip your Cover over your head and put it back in its purse ready to place straight back into your nappy bag or pram.

My opinion is that
anybody offended by breastfeeding
is staring too hard.

DAVID ALLEN, PRODUCTIVITY CONSULTANT/AUTHOR

*

Who fed me from her gentle breast

And hushed me in her arms to rest,

And on my cheek sweet kisses prest?

My Mother.

ANNE TAYLOR, POET

*

CHAPTER 3

Morphing into mum

No matter how much you fight it,
nature conspires against you
and it seems inevitable that you'll pick up
some of your mother's mannerisms.

HELLO, MUMMY!

Thou art thy mother's glass, and she in thee,

Calls back the lovely April of her prime.

WILLIAM SHAKESPEARE

❧

All women become like their mothers.
That is their tragedy.
No man does. That's his.

OSCAR WILDE, PLAYWRIGHT

❧

Contraction by contraction, the invisible cord pulls us tighter: moon, mother, daughter, baby. Thirty-two years apart, contraction by contraction, I am still linked to my mother. We are again sharing the childbirth bed as I am rocked in the same cradle of pain that saw me into the world. I have inherited the pattern of this labour from her. Fate had handed us the baton of this long, long race and now it is my turn to run with it.

ANNA MARIA DELL'OSO, AUTHOR

❧

Waiting at the traffic lights the other day, I glanced down at my hands as they rested on the steering wheel, and was struck by how much more like my mother's than my own they have suddenly become. Not that there's anything wrong with my mum's hands – it's just that hers are twenty years older than mine.

Driving into a car park a few minutes later, I asked the 'parking angel' if she could find me a space. It's barmy behaviour, I know, and the blame for it must sit firmly with my mother. I've heard her say the same thing so many times over the years that I am now powerless to resist repeating it, parrot fashion, whenever I enter a busy car park.

It wasn't until I got home, however, that the panic really set in. As I put the bin out, I asked the bird that regularly perches on the fence by our kitchen door how he was feeling today. 'Oh, Lord,' I wailed to my husband, when I got back inside. 'I've turned into my mother.'

RACHEL HALLIWELL, JOURNALIST

❧

65

She is roses, and London gardens, she is wartime movies, and Frank Sinatra songs, she is Italy and France, and China tea. She is soaked through everything I see. I look at my face in the mirror, at my mannerisms, the veins in my hands, and realise she will always be with me.

HARRIET WALTER, MOTHERS BY DAUGHTERS

ARE YOU MORPHING INTO YOUR MUM?

1. If your fabulous new shoes kill your feet, do you:

   (a) Decide not to wear them?
   (b) Battle on in the name of style?

2. When you buy a brand new frock, do you:

   (a) Look at the care label?
   (b) Look for new accessories to go with it?

3. Is a perfect night a:

   (a) Face pack, family-sized block of chocolate and the TV remote to yourself?
   (b) Bottle of wine, your girlfriends and take away

Mostly a's – Hello Mummy!
Mostly b's – One day you'll know what it's like (mutter in a mother's voice)

My mom is literally a part of me.
You can't say that about many people
except relatives, and organ donors.

CARRIE LATET, WRITER

MATCHING WRINKLES

A recent study found that mothers and daughters age in a strikingly similar pattern. State-of-the-art facial imaging and three-dimensional computer modelling was used to measure changes in the aging female face. The study found that volume loss in the lower eyelid began when women were in their mid-thirties and progressed steadily through life. If a mother demonstrated this type of sagging, then her daughter was likely to as well.

However, the sun continues to be identified as the number one cause of aging, so in this case Mum's largely off the hook. If you experience premature wrinkles it's not all, or even mostly, Mum's fault. You did it to yourself.

As I grow older I find myself becoming more and more like my mother, in appearance as well as in taste, independence and stubbornness … I even follow her lead in the hairdressing stakes, keeping, as she did, to the same colour and style.

JEAN THORNTON

MATCHING VOICES

When I read Beatrix Potter to Molly
I can hear my mother's intonations. And also
when I snap at her. And I wonder,
'Where did that parental voice come from?'

JANE CLIFTON, AUTHOR/ENTERTAINER

MATCHING LAUGHTER

I get my sense of humor from my mom. There are so many quiet times you spend as a mother that aren't glorified but are a foundation for your kids. No matter what, there was always a thick safety net under this trapeze.

TINA FEY, ACTRESS

HOW NOT TO MORPH INTO YOUR MOTHER

1. Never collect plastic bags, paper bags, or those twisty ties that come on bread packages.

2. Never buy, accept as a gift, or create yourself, a handmade anything that disguises toilet paper. We all know what's in there. .

3. Do not weed, mow the lawn, or sweep outside when it's thirty-five degrees plus because it will only take a moment and you know that your daughter/son has such a busy life.

4. Avoid saying, 'Did you want *that* haircut?'

5. When your children tell you something that they know as a fact, do not say in a doubting voice, 'I don't know'.

6. Don't tell a long involved story about how one of the cousins/neighbours is doing so well.

7. Don't tell a long involved story about someone that you've never heard of and never met, or have any desire to meet.

8. Refrain from asking your family gathered round the dining table to lift their feet while you dustbust underneath, as it only takes a couple of seconds to get rid of the crumbs.

9. Never, ever discuss the state of your bowels.

Be aware of your actions, and remember that your mother is probably waiting and hoping for the day you realise you have become her. Now go out and do something your mother would never do, and then send her flowers.

More than anything else, motherhood has given me a sense of the continuity of women that my understanding of feminism never gave me before. My sense of being connected, not just to my own mother but to generations of women is profound.

HANNIE RAYSON, PLAYWRIGHT

My daughters enlighten me about myself. Their presence acts as an ever-changing reflection of me as well as a source of feedback, as I see myself mirrored in their mannerisms, attitudes and relationships.

ELLEN A ROSEN, WRITER

If you can raise a child who can take part of your light, part of your gifts, part of what you've taught her and run like hell, nothing can bring you more joy.

GOLDIE HAWN, ACTRESS

CHAPTER 4

Colder than a mother-in-law's kiss

If you have a good relationship with your mother-in-law consider yourself to be very, very blessed. Many of us have a fraught relationship with the 'other woman' in the life of our partner.

A SIDE-EFFECT OF MARRIAGE

Never rely on the glory of the morning nor
the smiles of your mother-in-law.

JAPANESE PROVERB

❧

Of all the people I have studied,
from city dwellers to cave dwellers, I always find
that at least fifty per cent would prefer to have at
least one jungle between themselves and
their mother-in-law.

MARGARET MEAD, ANTHROPOLOGIST

❧

The Rodds have been wonderfully true to form – my
mother-in-law was told by the surgeon I should be in
danger for 3 days, & not one of them even rang up to
enquire let alone sending a bloom or anything. I long
to know if they bothered to look under R in the deaths
column, very much doubt it however.

LETTER FROM NANCY MITFORD (MARRIED NAME RODD)
to her sister Diana Moseley, after Nancy nearly died
from an ectopic pregnancy

❧

I should, many a good day, have blown my brains out, but for the recollection that it would have given pleasure to my mother-in-law; and, even then, if I could have been certain to haunt her – but I won't dwell upon these trifling family matters.

LORD BYRON, POET

ARE WOMEN PROGRAMMED TO DISLIKE THEIR MOTHER-IN-LAW?

Approximately two-thirds of Australian women claim that their mother-in-law causes them stress and anxiety. British psychologist Dr Terri Apter claims women are programmed to dislike their mother-in-law because of the persistent female stereotyping that continues to exist. Both the mother and wife are in a battle to achieve the same position in the family – the primary, most important woman.

Mothers-in-law expressed great disappointment at not being able to become friends with their daughters-in-law and were afraid that the poor relationship would alienate them from their sons and grandchildren. The sons appear to see their wives as stronger and will tend to sympathise with their mothers, which causes further trouble. Maybe husbands need to define each woman's role and help sort out the relationship with the mother and his wife, instead of standing aside and letting the women fight it out.

England's first female PM Baroness Thatcher, also known as the 'Iron Lady', was accused by her daughter-in-law of creating a mummy's boy. Soon after their marriage, Dianne and her husband Mark visited 10 Downing Street, the home of the ruling PM.

Said Dianne: 'Lady T hand-washed all of Mark's shirts, pressed them and folded them neatly in little plastic bags for travelling. Mark used to refer to moments like that as 'little spurts of mothering'. I don't think Mark ever left his mum. Her opinion mattered more than mine and he enjoyed her company more than mine.'

The marriage ended after eighteen years, following Mark's alleged involvement in a coup in Equatorial Guinea, which his mummy helped extricate him from.

I was never once allowed to visit the McMahon family house in Sydney. I had to sit in the car and wait for Julian while he visited his mother. She wanted nothing to do with me. I simply wasn't good enough.

DANNII MINOGUE SPEAKING OF HER FIRST MARRIAGE AND HER MOTHER-IN-LAW, SONIA MCMAHON

-&

I told my mother-in-law

that my house was her house,

and she said:

'Get the hell off my property'.

JOAN RIVERS, COMEDIAN

-&

Every man must define his identity against his mother. If he does not, he just falls back into her and is swallowed up.

CAMILLE PAGLIA, AUTHOR

TRYING TO GET ALONG
WITH THE MOTHER-IN-LAW

An anxious-to-please Marilyn Monroe visited her future mother-in-law with her fiancé, playwright Arthur Miller. They dined in Mrs Miller's tiny apartment and all proceeded smoothly. Just before the engaged couple left, Marilyn needed to use the facilities. A flimsy bathroom door was the only thing between her and the living room.

To avoid embarrassment, Marilyn took the precaution of turning on the taps fully, and soon rejoined her fiancé and mother-in-law to be. The next day Arthur phoned his mother and asked, 'How did you like her?' His mother replied, 'She's sweet. A wonderful, wonderful girl but she pees like a horse.'

A GREEN MOTHER-IN-LAW

Mother-in-law's Tongue (or Snake Plant) is a good pick for people who have no luck growing houseplants. It survives in low to bright light, and requires very little water to stay healthy. It is a perfect choice for people who tend to neglect houseplants, since this plant is hard to kill. However, it can be dangerous. Keep this plant away from pets and small children, as it is toxic if eaten.

MOTHERING MOTHERS-IN-LAW

Edgar Allen Poe formed an intense attachment to his mother-in-law, Marie Clemm. He was buried between her, his beloved 'Muddy', and his wife, Virginia. He wrote this sonnet to attempt to express his feelings and gratitude towards her.

To my mother

Because the angels in the Heaven above,

    Devoutly singing unto one another,

Can find, amid their burning terms of love,

    None so devotional as that of 'mother,'

Therefore by that sweet name I long have called you:

    In setting my Virginia's spirit free.

My mother — my own mother, who died early,

    Was but the mother of myself; but you

Are mother to the dead I loved so dearly,

    Are thus more precious than the one I knew,

By that infinity with which my wife

    Was dearer to my soul than its soul-life.

MOTHER-IN-LAW

To my Mother-in-Law,

Finding in the attic the bundle of hemp cloth you used to raise the nine children and that you left behind, I thought of your sigh as you lamented the synthetic fabric they would spin out now like your hemp cloth, and I felt the tears start. You made the cosy baby blanket for my first baby, with the cotton you asked from a villager who grew it on the small side of a mountain. That baby is now grown taller than I and his thick black hair, seen from the back, is exactly as yours used to be.

When I was filled with anxiety watching my children sleep, you told me that I know your heart and that you know mine, but you left my side before I was old enough, wise enough to really understand your heart. Even though the tooth you lost every time you gained a child made chewing difficult, you loved zucchini pancakes; now, every time I prepare zucchini pancakes, the lump in my throat keeps me from swallowing. When the afternoon drowsiness flooded in, you put two pillows side-by-side and told the long-ago stories of your son, my husband, as if there would be, could be, no end, but when will you hear the stories that have piled up since you left our side?

Putting your hand, rough as arrowroot brambles, on the inner flesh still white and soft, you looked at your hand I saw in your eyes our lack of devotion, but it was too late to revoke your sorrow. On the day when the family heir was born, you held him in your arms and asked him where he had been. And where are you now?

In the snow and in the rain, in the alternate rise and fall of the sun and the moon, your expression was always hardened, but stepping out from the front door with the first child on your back, bent with years of hardship, where did you get such light feet, such bursts of joyous energy?

Your smile as you told me that the new baby of our house has a heel softer than an egg has inspired my patience. The day you left, my white mourning dress wound around the coffin and would not let go.

In the midst of time that allows neither going nor coming, you and I have separated, but in the taste of the bean paste of our house, your heart is still deeply buried.

LEE SOOK-JUNG, WRITER

SMOTHERING MOTHER-IN-LAWS

Conscience is a mother-in-law
whose visit never ends.

❧

My wife is the kind of girl
who will not go anywhere without her mother,
and her mother will go anywhere.

❧

Lord John Russell, on being asked what he would consider
a proper punishment for bigamy:
Two mothers-in-law.

❧

Give up all hope of peace
so long as your mother-in-law is alive.

JUVENAL, POET AD 1

❧

PENTHERAPHOBIA

The profound fear of the mother-in-law.

Symptoms

- Dread • Air hunger
- Elevated or irregular heart rates • Trembling
- Intimidation • Anger • Nausea • Sweating

This phobia can present problems within a marriage because while there is a struggle to establish your own family, at the same time there seems to be this invisible, but ever-present cord that ties your response to the dictations of a mother-in-law.

Cure

The mother-in-law may have the best opportunity to lessen the fear. One suggested ritual is for the mother-in-law to offer her new daughter- or son-in-law an apron with the strings cut. This symbolises the mother-in-law's wish to demonstrate her intentions to remain hands off in her child's new marriage. This can provide great relief to the bride who may wonder how strong that bond may continue to be.

Another possible solution is to seek help and sometimes intervention with a therapist who can help you learn ways to manage your fear and skills to establish your own home apart from the undue influence of your mother-in-law.

●

British writer, Anna Pasternak, writes how she assumed any potential mother-in-law would welcome her with a wide smile and open cashmere-clad arms as other boyfriends' mothers had done in the past. Instead her future mother-in-law served her over-cooked offal for lunch with a tight grimace.

A few weeks later, we met for 'drinkie poos' at their home and toasted our future happiness with lukewarm 'cham-poo' and Pringles from the packet – classy. When we went to the local pub for supper, his mother took charge of the seating plan. Her son was next to her and I was put opposite. It is one of the biggest regrets of my life, apart from accepting the blind date with my ex in the first place, that I did not speak up then at what was a brilliantly subtle piece of social engineering.

Worse, as if further staking her maternal hold, his mother spent the entire evening running her hands through her son's fringe and proprietorially clutching his arm as though he were about twelve – which, given the state of his bedroom before I got hold of it, appeared to be what she thought he still was.

Needless to say, she expressed her state of mourning at the wedding by wearing black, albeit with a few gold leaves embroidered on for good measure. She also gave me a piece of family jewellery after the wedding – a silver shark's tooth necklace – and announced: 'This is an anti-feminist necklace because you have to get a man to undo it.'

It was indeed fearsomely tight, so much so that I was convinced she was trying to strangle me. Wearing it gave me a splitting headache, and I remember asking my ex to pull over on the hard shoulder of the motorway on the way home and take it off me. I was tempted to throw it out of the window, but didn't for fear that I would be arrested for smashing a passing windscreen.

◆

A husband always prefers
his wife's mother-in-law
to his own.

ANONYMOUS

HOW TO MOTHER-IN-LAW PROOF YOUR HOME

Feng shui will work better if you try to make a transformation in your attitude.

In your own home:

1. Be welcoming to your mother-in-law.

2. Light up the south-west corner of your lounge room with a bright light and place a flattering picture of both of you – wife and mother-law – smiling happily, in the corner. Choose a large picture so both of you can see it and be reminded of how close you are or can be.

3. Place two crystal balls on a table, also in the south-west corner. This creates excellent Earth energy that will help both of you to bond well.

4. If there continues to be tensions, paint a wall red. Fire element energy is always effective for burning up feelings of hostility and tension.

5. If possible, have grandchildren. The energy of children is pure and very yang, which helps dissolve conflict and disharmony.

If you stay with your mother-in-law:

This situation is much more difficult because it's likely your mother-in-law will exert a great deal of authority.

1. Wear a powerful amulet that will help reduce any feelings of hostility. A rooster with amethysts is excellent. Carry it always.

2. Place two crystal balls on a table where both you and your mother-in-law can see them. This may help ameliorate any tension or leftover anger.

◆

But there, everything has its drawbacks,

as the man said when his mother-in-law died,

and they came down upon him

for the funeral expenses.

JEROME K JEROME, AUTHOR

IF YOU CAN'T BEAT THEM, JOIN THEM

Alan Monks married his mother-in-law Valerie in 1985, and his former wife Jeanette who is Valerie's daughter, was the bridesmaid.

Alan says, 'She was a great mother-in-law, but she's been even better as my wife … I'm still head over heels in love with her. And it's made my life a lot easier that Jeanette has been so supportive.'

After Jeanette and Alan divorced, Valerie agreed to look after Alan and her grandchildren for six months, while Jeanette kept the family home. Gradually, Valerie and Alan fell in love and Alan proposed. They could only marry after they presented the case for their marriage before both Houses of Westminster. They were granted an Act of Parliament to go ahead and wed, overcoming a 400-year-old law laid down by Henry VIII that banned marriages between men and their mothers-in-law.

Jeanette, Alan's ex-wife and stepdaughter and Valerie's daughter, who is still single says, 'I only wish Mum had met him before I did so they could have been together longer. They're my two favourite people in the world.'

HOAX OR NOT — IT'S STILL A JOKE

Barnet Council in the UK denied that they had outlawed mother-in-law jokes, despite media reports that the council had implemented such a ban.

The council claimed that it did create a handout stating that mother-in-law jokes were 'offensively sexist' and disrespectful to 'family elders', however this handout was only intended for staff members who attended a 'one off' equality and diversity training session. Council advised its staff to be 'polite' to all members of the public.

◆

Behind every successful man
stands a surprised mother-in-law.

VOLTAIRE, PHILOSOPHER/WRITER

◆

They say the definition of ambivalence
is watching your mother-in-law
drive over a cliff in your new Cadillac.

DAVID MAMET, PLAYWRIGHT

◆

Only Adam had no mother-in-law.

That's how we know he lived in paradise.

OLD YIDDISH SAYING

❧

This young Dublin fella comes home all excited to tell his ma he's fallen in love and going to get married. He says: 'Just for fun, Ma, I'm going to bring over three women and you just try and guess which one I'm going to marry.'

The mother agrees, so the next day he brings along three beautiful women and sits them down on the couch and they chat away for a while. He then says: 'Right, OK Ma, guess which one I'm going to marry.'

She immediately replies, 'The one in the middle.'

'That's amazing, Ma. You're right. How did ye know?'

'I don't like her.'

❧

CHAPTER 5

Mothers in the house

Houses get dirty and clothes need to be washed.
Often it seems to be the mother's responsibility
whether she wants it or not.

THE WORK THAT NEVER ENDS

Housework can't kill you, but why take a chance?

PHYLLIS DILLER, COMEDIAN

❧

My idea of housework is to
sweep the room with a glance.

ANONYMOUS

❧

It's so easy to keep women happy. If you [men] do a bit more

housework, you'll get more sex. It's a simple equation.

KATHY LETTE, AUTHOR

❧

I'm not going to vacuum
'til Sears makes one you can ride on.

ROSEANNE BARR, COMEDIAN

MARRIED TO THE HOUSE

Home is the girl's prison and the
woman's workhouse.

GEORGE BERNARD SHAW, PLAYWRIGHT

❧

As soon as she had the house to herself, she got to work. She did all the washing in the basket and stripped the beds and washed all the bedding. She did the blankets today as well as the sheets and got them all out on the line without needing to tilt her head up. It took a long time, but my word it was satisfying to see them all out purifying in the sun.

Then she got down on her hands and knees to scrub the kitchen floor. It was amazing how much dirt could come off even the cleanest-looking floor when you got down and scrubbed at it. It was the corners especially, of course, and the little cracks where the cupboards joined the floor. She got out an old toothbrush – well, it was Hugh's, she would get him a new one – and got into all the cracks with it, using lots of cleaner, smelling the lemons in it, watching the foam grow brown.

What a good feeling it was, sponging off the dirt, pouring the water away down the sink! Just to make sure, she filled the bucket again with clean water to sponge it all over. Even the second time she thought a bit more dirt came off, so she did it again. So much dirt, hiding in her kitchen, all along, when she thought it was clean!

KATE GRENVILLE, *THE IDEA OF PERFECTION*

STICK THIS UP ON YOUR FRIDGE

At worst, a house unkempt cannot be so distressing as a life unlived.

ROSE MACAULAY, AUTHOR

REASONS TO BE GRATEFUL

Hang this above your sparkling white automatic washer and feel grateful for some progress.

- Build a fire in your backyard to heat a kettle of rain water.

- Set the tubs so smoke won't blow in eyes if wind is sharp.

- Shave one whole cake of lye soap in boiling water.

- Sort things. Make three piles: one pile white, one pile coloured, one pile work britches and rags.

- Stir flour in cold water 'til smooth, then thin down with boiling water for starching.

- Rub dirty spots on board, scrub hard, boil. Rub coloureds but don't boil, just rinse and starch.

- Take white things out of kettle with broomstick handle, then rinse, blue and starch.

- Spread tea towels on grass.

- Hang old rags on fence.

- Pour rinse water on flower beds.

- Scrub porch with hot, soapy water.

- Go put on a clean dress, smooth hair with side-combs, brew cup of tea, sit and rest and rock a spell, and count blessings.

ANONYMOUS

LOVING HOUSEWORK

It is a privilege to prepare the place
where someone else will sleep.

ELIZABETH JOLLEY, AUTHOR

❧

[I]… thought of my mother, how she would clean up after me when as a child I had what she called a 'bilious attack'. I remember her patience in the middle of the night, the precious moments of her attention, in the house full of sleeping children who had usurped my place in her affections. In a trance of gratitude I would watch her spread the clean sheet across the bed, stretch it flat and tuck in its corners, making it nice again for the disgusting, squalid creature I had become. Without revulsion, she would pick up the soiled sheets in her arms and bear them away.

HELEN GARNER, *THE SPARE ROOM*

RANDOM HOUSEHOLD TIPS THAT WORK

We've all heard that you should clean the bathroom every day and then it will supposedly never need cleaning. The suggestion is that every time you have a shower you should wipe it down afterwards with your towel. All a bit too much work, and being a Dame Wash-a-lot, I would end up needing to wash the towel because who wants to dry themselves with a towel used to wipe down tiles. My grandmother always said make the beds, keep the floor clear, and people will think you're tidy. You can also try these hints:

- *Want to get rid of cockroaches?* Fill an aluminium foil tray with a mixture of ½ bicarbonate soda and ½ sugar. Place the tray somewhere that children and pets won't be near. The mixture will cause terrible things to happen to the insides of the cockroaches – and no more cockroaches!

- *Mouse repellent.* When mice invade your home, put out sacks of crushed peppermint leaves to chase them away. Make them by filling old stockings, socks or pantyhose with peppermint leaves (from your garden or from your local health food store). Mice dislike the smell and stay away. You can also try dribbling peppermint oil around the skirting boards.

- *Microfibre cloths do work!* Dampen them and you'll remove bacteria from surfaces.

- *Save the car.*   Suspend a tennis ball from the garage ceiling and when the windscreen touches the ball your bumper is two centimetres from the wall.

- *Are your shoes too tight?*   Put on two pairs of socks, and squeeze your feet into the shoes (this is the tricky part), then blast your feet with your hairdryer.

- *Don't make a monkey of yourself.*   Pull bananas apart before displaying them in your fruit bowl. If you leave them connected at the stem, they'll ripen faster and go brown quicker.

- *Got a small dint on the car?*   Place the bathroom plunger over it, and gently push it in and out. Some-times this actually works.

- *Blunt scissors?*   Cut ten times through three sheets of tin foil. Repeat after testing, if necessary.

- *Keep drains clean.*   Once a month, drop three antacid tablets, followed by a cup of plain white vinegar, down the drain in your kitchen. Then wait a few minutes and run the hot water. The combination of acid and bubbles will dissolve any food or grease stuck in the pipes.

- *Does the gunk left by a sticky price tag annoy you?*   Turn a hairdryer on low and aim it at the tag. Gently peel it off and no mess will be left.

- *Saggy celery?*   Pop it in a jug of water, and it will revive.

LOATHING HOUSEWORK

Man is made for something
better than disturbing dust.

OSCAR WILDE, PLAYWRIGHT

❧

When it comes to housework, the one thing no book
of household management can ever tell you is how to
begin. Or maybe I mean why?

KATHERINE WHITEHORN, JOURNALIST

❧

I hate housework!
You make the beds, you do the dishes – and six
months later you have to start all over again.

JOAN RIVERS, COMEDIAN

THREE-SECOND RULE

This so-called rule says that food you have dropped on
the ground is OK to eat if you pick it up in three seconds
or less. This rule is applied especially to delicious food.

Unfortunately, it's not true. Bacteria can attach to your
food as soon as it hits the ground. Moist food, such as
cake, picks up bacteria even more easily.

IT CAN GRIND YOU DOWN

Cleaning your house
while your kids are still growing up
is like shovelling the walk
before it stops snowing.

PHYLLIS DILLER, COMEDIAN

❧

My second favourite household chore is ironing.
My first being hitting my head on the top bunk
until I faint.

ERMA BOMBECK, HUMORIST

❧

I think housework is far more tiring and frightening
than hunting is, no comparison, and yet after hunting
we had eggs for tea and were made to rest for hours, but
after housework people expect one to go on just as if
nothing special had happened.

NANCY MITFORD, *PURSUIT OF LOVE*

THINGS I'VE LEARNED

The best way to cut pizza is with scissors.

You can dry socks in the microwave.

When buying socks, buy two identical pairs at a time:
then you have to lose three before you have an odd sock.

When in doubt, just give money.

Just when you think you've gone too far, go further.

You can feed toddlers in the bath.

If you have a toothpaste stain on a black dress just colour
it in with black texta.

If you need to talk on the phone and you have three
children under four, just sit them on a blanket, give them
a spoon each and plonk a giant Milo tin in the middle.

You don't need air-conditioning in a car; if it's hot just give
each person a spray bottle filled with water.

When you have three little boys at a check-out and you
are halfway through a $300 load of shopping and one
needs a wee, ask the check-out chick for two plastic bags,
put one inside another, tell everyone to close their eyes,
and make like a disposable urinal.

CATHERINE DEVENY, AUTHOR/COMEDIAN

CHAPTER 6

Remarkable mothers

All mothers are remarkable;
here are some stories
of what mothers can do.

THE MOTHERS OF INVENTION

Plato said, 'Necessity is the mother of invention'. Here are some inventions by mothers in answer to some practical problems.

- Frustrated with the endless need to change her youngest child's soiled cloth nappies, bed sheets and clothing, Marion Donovan sat down at her sewing machine with a shower curtain and created a waterproof nappy cover. Next she used strong and absorbent paper that kept water away from the baby's skin to create the disposable nappy.

- Mary Phelps Jacob decided she had had enough of whalebone and steel-rod corsets. She took two silk handkerchiefs and sewed them together using pink ribbon and cord. Voila – the brassiere!

- Bette Nesmith Graham (mother of Monkee, Mike Nesmith), a secretary, had to retype entire pages if she made one small error. She observed how window painters simply brushed over their mistake with a fresh coat of paint. With a dab of white, water-based tempera paint she covered her typing errors and 'Liquid Paper' was born.

BRAVE MUMS

There are many brave mums out there.

They keep moving forward one step at a time, while all the time loving their children under circumstances that only they will know. My granny lost her thirteen-year-old son, and even though every single day of her life she felt a gaping Jack-shaped hole, she was still full of joy and love. She kept walking forward.

❧

Sometimes the strength of motherhood
is greater than natural laws.

BARBARA KINGSOLVER, AUTHOR

❧

A woman is like a teabag.
Only when in hot water
do you realise how strong she is.

NANCY REAGAN, WIFE OF EX US PRESIDENT RONALD REAGAN

... She thinks how she fought a flood during her husband's absence. She stood for hours in the drenching downpour, and dug an overflow gutter to save the dam across the creek. But she could not save it. There are things that a bushwoman cannot do. Next morning the dam was broken, and her heart was nearly broken too, for she thought how her husband would feel when he came home and saw the result of years of labour swept away. She cried then.

She also fought the pleuro-pneumonia – dosed and bled the few remaining cattle, and wept again when her two best cows died.

Again, she fought a mad bullock that besieged the house for a day. She made bullets and fired at him through cracks in the slabs with an old shot-gun. He was dead in the morning. She skinned him and got seventeen-and-sixpence for the hide.

She also fights the crows and eagles that have designs on her chickens. Her plan of campaign is very original. The children cry 'Crows, mother!' and she rushes out and aims a broomstick at the birds as though it were a gun, and says 'Bung!' The crows leave in a hurry; they are cunning, but a woman's cunning is greater.

Occasionally a bushman in the horrors, or a villainous-looking sundowner, comes and nearly scares the life out of her. She generally tells the suspicious-looking stranger that her husband and two sons are at work below the dam, or over at the yard, for he always cunningly inquires for the boss.

Only last week a gallows-faced swagman – having satisfied himself that there were no men on the place – threw his swag down on the veranda, and demanded tucker. She gave him something to eat; then he expressed the intention of staying for the night. It was sundown then. She got a batten from the sofa, loosened the dog, and confronted the stranger, holding the batten in one hand and the dog's collar with the other. 'Now you go!' she said. He looked at her and at the dog, said 'All right, mum,' in a cringing tone and left. She was a determined-looking woman, and Alligator's yellow eyes glared unpleasantly – besides, the dog's chewing-up apparatus greatly resembled that of the reptile he was named after.

She has few pleasures to think of as she sits here alone by the fire, on guard against a snake. All days are much the same for her; but on Sunday afternoon she dresses herself, tidies the children, smartens up baby, and goes for a lonely walk along the bush-track, pushing an old perambulator in front of her. She does this every Sunday. She takes as much care to make herself and the children look smart as she would if she were going to do the block in the city. There is nothing to see, however, and not a soul to meet. You might walk for twenty miles along this track without being able to fix a point in your mind, unless you are a bushman. This is because of the everlasting, maddening sameness of the stunted trees – that monotony which makes a man long to break away and travel as far as trains can go, and sail as far as ship can sail – and farther.

HENRY LAWSON, *THE DROVER'S WIFE*

MUMS WHO PROTECT
OTHER PEOPLE'S CHILDREN

Irena Sendler, a young Catholic mother, saved the lives of about 2500 Jewish children in the Warsaw ghetto during World War II. Using the codename 'Jolanta', and wearing a Star of David armband to identify herself with the Jewish population, Sendler became part of an escape network. One baby was spirited away in a mechanic's toolbox; some children were transported in coffins, suitcases and sacks; and others escaped through the city's sewer system. An ambulance driver who smuggled infants under stretchers in the back of his van kept his dog on the seat beside him, having trained the animal to bark to mask any cries from his hidden passengers.

Sendler kept a list of the names of all the children she saved, in the hope that she could one day reunite them with their families. The Nazis captured and tortured her, but Sendler didn't reveal how, when the Germans surrounded her house, she threw the roll of names to a colleague who hid it in her underwear.

Get away from her,

you bitch!

RIPLEY (SIGOURNEY WEAVER) to the giant
egg-laying alien queen. The alien is about to kill Newt,
Ripley's young quasi-daughter, *Aliens*

MOTHERS WHO DON'T FORGET

In the mid-eighteenth century, babies were accepted anonymously into the Foundling Hospital to avoid the mothers being publicly shamed into abandoning their babies elsewhere. A sign instructed the mother to leave a small token pinned to her baby, so if circumstances changed the woman could reclaim the 'right' child.

These tokens included metal hearts, ribbons, fabric scraps and baby clothes. One cut her child's shirt in two, retaining half. Another deposited one sleeve with her baby and kept the other. Mothers left hearts drawn on paper, metal hearts, embroidered hearts and hearts cut out in fabric.

Some mothers did reclaim their children. Sarah Bender attached a piece of elaborate patchwork, made up of bits of printed fabric on which she had embroidered a heart in red thread. She retained the matching piece. Almost ten years later, she revisited the Foundling Hospital and presented her piece of patchwork. Her son Charles Benjamin was returned to her.

Children are the anchors
that hold a mother to life.

SOPHOCLES, ANCIENT GREEK PLAYWRIGHT

CHAPTER 7

Working
mums

Many mothers complain of being tired.
It's no wonder when you realise how much
the average mother does.

WORKING MUMS

A man's work is from sun to sun,
but a mother's work is never done.

ANONYMOUS

❦

By and large, mothers and housewives are the only
workers who do not have regular time off. They are
the great vacation-less class.

ANNE MORROW LINDBERGH, AVIATOR/WRITER

❦

Working mothers are guinea pigs
in a scientific experiment to show that
sleep is not necessary to human life.

ANONYMOUS

❦

Any mother could perform the jobs of
several air traffic controllers with ease.

LISA ALTHER, AUTHOR

LOVING YOUR WORK

The time you spend outside the home really refreshes you.
It's like a blood transfusion.

KATE LANGBROEK, BROADCASTER/WRITER

❧

It has to work for my family,
otherwise I can't do the job.

CATE BLANCHETT, ACTRESS

❧

Many people have said to me, 'What a pity you had such a big family to raise. Think of the novels and the short stories and the poems you never had time to write because of that.' And I looked at my children and I said, 'These are my poems. These are my short stories.'

OLGA MASTERS, AUTHOR

❧

I'd just given birth, so I was like, 'OK, I'm [still] a woman – I want to do this film.' And I do have a life other than simply feeding this baby. I think when you give birth you get itchy to get back to work and you want to feel life still goes on.

NICOLE KIDMAN, ACTRESS

WORKING WITH GUILT

Who comes first?

I'd like to say it's always them, but sometimes it's not. And here's where the guilt creeps in … Am I being selfish for occasionally putting myself first? Sometimes they have to go to day-care or after-school care because I'm working. The guilt on those days is horrendous. It's not made any better by the fact that my two-year-old daughter cries most mornings when I drop her off at day-care. Though several minutes later she's perfectly fine, it's the crying when I leave that makes me feel depressed and guilty. Am I damaging her irreparably? Or is she just 'putting it on'?

I don't think I'll ever know.

ALEESAH DARLISON, AUTHOR

❧

At work you think of the children you have left at home. At home you think of the work you've left unfinished. Such a struggle is unleashed within yourself. Your heart is rent.

GOLDA MEIR, EX ISRAELI PRIME MINISTER

❧

I was standing in the schoolyard waiting for a child when another mother came up to me. 'Have you found work yet?' she asked. 'Or are you still just writing.'

ANNE TYLER, AUTHOR

❧

CHAPTER 8

Motherchef

The hub of the house is the kitchen.
The hub of the kitchen is mum.

MUMS IN THE KITCHEN

The most remarkable thing
about my mother is that for thirty years
she served my family leftovers.
The original has never been found.

CALVIN TRILLIN, JOURNALIST/HUMORIST

❧

My mother was a great believer in child labour.

BRITISH FOOD WRITER NIGELLA LAWSON
STARTED COOKING EARLY

❧

In general,
my children refused to eat anything
that hadn't danced on TV.

ERMA BOMBECK, HUMORIST

THE FIFTIES — THE WAR IS OVER, BUT THE COOKING'S STILL PLAIN

After World War II, the world was still uncertain. Food became more plentiful but mums tended to stick to the recipes they knew. Roasts for main courses, junkets for dessert, and cakes that their mothers made. Some mums continued with their wartime recipes.

Dripping Cake

4 oz self-raising flour	3 oz sugar
pinch of salt	1 reconstituted dried egg
1 teaspoon mixed spice	milk and water to mix
3 oz clarified dripping	

Sift flour, salt and mixed spice. Rub in the dripping. Add remainder of ingredients with enough milk and water to make a sticky consistency. Put into a greased and floured 7 inch tin. Bake in a moderate oven for about 1 hour.

THE SIXTIES – IT'S IN THE CAN

The sixties liberated the cooks to have more time to wear kaftans, dance to the Beatles and put some flowers in their hair. We watched *The Jetsons*, *Lost in Space* and *Star Trek*. We teetered on the edge of a new frontier, holding a can opener in our hand. Forget about the Age of Aquarius, it was the Age of Can Cooking.

Crab chowder

1 can tomato soup

1 can celery soup

1 can asparagus soup

1 can crab meat

½ can milk

1 diced potato

1 diced onion

Fry onion and diced potato, then add all other ingredients. Heat, but be careful not to bring to boil.

Ambrosia

1 can mandarins

1 can pineapple pieces

1 cup sultana grapes

1 packet marshmallows

1 cup coconut

300 g sour cream

Chop and drain fruit and marshmallows.

Mix all ingredients and leave overnight in refrigerator.

THE SEVENTIES – IT'S A HIP HAPPENING TIME

Mothers got into dinner parties. The women dressed up in pantsuits and the men donned cravats and safari suits. Cosmopolitan cooking had arrived.

How to host a fondue party

Fondue parties are easy, fun, and make socialising a snap, even for a busy party host. They are intimate and social times, which allow the guests to eat food in close quarters.

• Keep melted cheese or broth hot in your fondue pot. Skewer foods such as meats, bread cubes and vegetables. These can be either cooked in the liquid, or simply dipped in.

• For dessert – why not try melted chocolate? Dip in cake cubes and fruit.

• Everyone loves a fondue party!

And afterwards, mums and dads pulled out the Twister mat. It was 'the game that ties you into knots!'

THE EIGHTIES — NOUVEAU CUISINE
FOLLOWED BY DECADENT FEASTS

Early in the eighties, mums and dads returned from restaurants with growling stomachs. No-one can forget the disappointment of the waiter presenting you with a huge white plate dotted with an exquisite, architecturally constructed morsel as big as a sardine. Nouveau cuisine was rapidly replaced with 'posh nosh'. Mothers embraced the chance to create what they sampled in restaurants.

Piña colada   (Serves 4)

500 ml (2 cups) chilled pineapple juice

125 ml (½ cup) white rum

125 ml (½ cup) coconut cream

2 tablespoons finely chopped palm sugar

1 cup crushed ice

crushed ice, extra, to serve

Place pineapple juice, rum, coconut cream, palm sugar and ice in the jug of a blender and blend until smooth. Transfer to a serving jug and serve immediately over crushed ice.

CHAPTER 9

Mummy types

*Fashions in motherhood are constantly evolving.
Victorian mothers believed that 'Children
should be seen and not heard'. In the 1920s,
a scientific approach was applied to motherhood.
In the 1960s, hippie mums named their children
after the elements of the Earth – Skye,
Rainbow and River. In every era,
a new type of mother appears.*

During the 1990s a new species of mummy appeared. Soon after giving birth she emerges with all traces of pregnancy erased, except for the stylish little baby she totes on her hip or in the latest pram. The yummy mummy is immaculate, yoga slim, stylish and sexually attractive. No patches of baby sick festoon the yummy mummy's top, and no dark circles shadow her eyes. The ultimate compliment you can pay a yummy mummy is, 'You look amazing and not at all like you've just had a baby.'

Famous yummy mummies

- Sarah Murdoch
- Cate Blanchett
- Angelina Jolie
- Gwen Stefani
- Jennifer Lopez
- Elle Macpherson
- Nicole Kidman
- Princess Mary
- Bec Hewitt
- Erica Packer
- Dannii Minogue

SLUMMY MUMMIES

We've all seen yummy mummies at school pick-ups when they waft up to the gate looking unhurried, immaculately groomed and well-rested. But for those of us unable to afford or want the household help and designer accessories that would aid our ascent to yummy mummydom, we can embrace being a slummy mummy.

She's the mother whose children arrive at school wearing odd socks and with their swimming kit still sitting on the kitchen table. Her home totters uncertainly between shabby chic and just plain shabby ... When she gets back from the school run, she thinks about doing some yoga, but she puts the telly on instead. Slummy mummy does not shirk her maternal responsibilities, although she is liable to take a few short cuts for the sake of her own sanity ... She is human and fallible and, most importantly, likeable.

LOWRIE TURNER, JOURNALIST

—

Sometimes it is a question of getting through the days, but then from nowhere come those moments that you want to preserve forever.

FIONA NEILL, *SLUMMY MUMMY*

CHAPTER 10

Mother and child

When you hold your baby for the first time, love floods through you. Often this is swiftly followed by panic. You are no longer only responsible for yourself. I remember breaking out in a sweat as I struggled to master the hospital's highly complicated way of folding nappies. The totally irrational thought filled me that the hospital wouldn't let me take my daughter home if I couldn't fold the nappy properly.

Bitter are the tears of a child: Sweeten them.

Deep are the thoughts of a child: Quiet them.

Sharp is the grief of a child: Take it from him.

Soft is the heart of a child: Do not harden it.

LADY PAMELA GLENCONNER, AUTHOR

❧

A soiled baby, with a neglected nose,
cannot be conscientiously regarded
as a thing of beauty.

MARK TWAIN, AUTHOR/HUMORIST

❧

One of the biggest complaints about motherhood is the
lack of training. We all come to it armed only with a
phone number for a diaper service, a polaroid camera,
a hotline to the paediatrician, and an innocence with
a lifespan of fifteen minutes.

ERMA BOMBECK, HUMORIST

❧

A child is a curly dimpled lunatic.

RALPH WALDO EMERSON, POET/ESSAYIST

SLEEPING BABIES

Newborn babies are meant to sleep for sixteen to eighteen hours a day, and for one to three hours at a stretch. Many babies obviously don't seem to know what they're meant to do.

❧

… I'd certainly forgotten that sleep deprivation is a sophisticated form of torture used by repressive regimes to control dissidents, and by newborn babies to control their mothers.

PAT McDERMOTT, JOURNALIST/HUMORIST

❧

I think motherhood makes you apathetic because you're always so tired. I don't know how anyone can march or be politically active when they've only had three hours' sleep.

JO BRAND, COMEDIAN

SLEEPY OR DEAF DADS

A British survey revealed only a quarter of men wake up when the baby cries, and a fifth wake up once the mother is already awake. Half of fathers sleep on, or at least pretend to, when their baby cries in the middle of the night.

SLEEPLESS NIGHTS

There was never a child so lovely,
but his mother was glad to get him asleep.

RALPH WALDO EMERSON, POET/ESSAYIST

❧

The child cries. It has long been hoarse and weak from crying, but still it cries, and who can say when it will be comforted? And Varka wants to sleep. Her eyelids droop, her head hangs, her neck pains her. She can hardly move her eyelids or her lips, and it seems to her that her face is sapless and petrified, and that her head has shrivelled up to the size of a pinhead.

ANTON CHEKHOV, *SLEEPY*

❧

People who say they sleep like a baby

usually don't have one.

LEO BURKE, WRITER

❧

I actually remember feeling delight, at two o'clock in the morning, when the baby woke for his feed, because I so longed to have another look at him.

MARGARET DRABBLE, AUTHOR

IN-THE-MIDDLE-OF-THE-NIGHT MOTHERS

- During the night, keep your baby's room as dark and quiet as possible (babies don't need total dark or quiet to sleep).
- Use a dim light when you need to attend to baby during the night.
- At night, respond to baby's cries quickly, and settle or feed as soon as you can.
- You might also want to give night feeds in your baby's room. This will help keep night feeds brief, and make them different from daytime feeds.
- Play and talk after a feed is good during the day. But at night, adopt a soothing, quiet approach to interacting with your baby. Keep play for daytime.

RAISING CHILDREN NETWORK AUSTRALIA

❧

Some of the tenderest times I have spent with my little one is nursing in the dark, with everything quiet and her little hand caressing just below my neck. Her little eyes are closed and it's like the two of us are in our own little world. I wouldn't trade these moments for anything …

except maybe a full night's sleep!

NICKI HESKIN, JOURNALIST/PARENT EDUCATOR

❧

a police siren
from the distant highway
baby cries for her feed

MARY HIND, POET

❧

I creep into her room and stare down at her. Smooth baby skin, beautiful sleeping face and soft, downy fair hair. I'd rather look than pick her up, my brand new daughter – I'm still scared I'll harm her with my awkwardness.

NICOLE SWAIN, WRITER

❧

MAKING THE MOST OF BEING A MIDDLE-OF-THE-NIGHT MOTHER

Stephenie Meyer wrote bestselling *Twilight* in three months after she dreamt the plot. She wrote, barely sleeping, typing one-handed with a baby in her lap. 'I know to the day when I became a writer. One day. Which is cool. I can't close doors and write. Even if the kids are asleep, I know that I could hear them if I needed. I feel better if I'm kind of in the centre of things and I know what's going on.'

TOILET TRAINING

During the 1920s, a highly regimented approach to infant care was mass-marketed. Under such systems cleanliness took precedence over affection, and all aspects of child-rearing, including potty-training, were subject to strict timetables. Potty-training was to begin at around two months and the baby was encouraged to perform regular bowel evacuations at the same time each day, aided by a salt-water enema, if necessary.

WHO WINS AT NAPPY CHANGING?

- Women take two minutes and five seconds.

- Men take one minute and thirty-six seconds.

- Men lay out everything beforehand and whizz through the nappy change.

- Women tend to play and bond with the babies during a nappy change.

After sponsoring the research, Tesco the UK supermarket chain has decided to stock nappies in the DIY sections of some of its stores.

❧

What comes into play is the smell factor.
The worse the smell, the quicker you change
the nappy. Men don't like to hang about.

Jonathan Coleman, television and radio personality

❧

CHAPTER 11

Mum's the word

Most mothers seem to have a lot to say.
We all vow that we'll never say things like our
mothers said to our children, but it's as if it's
imprinted on mother DNA. Words fly out
of our mouths before we can shut
our lips to trap them.

My mother says, I never should

play with the gypsies in the woods.

If I did, she would say,

naughty, naughty girl to disobey.

Traditional

WHAT MOTHERS SAY

Hygienic mums
- Did you wash your hands?
- Don't put that in your mouth, you don't know where it's been.
- If you suck your thumb, it will drop off.
- If you pick your nose, it will bleed.
- If you pick your nose, you'll poison your brain.
- If you pick a pimple, it will scar.

Empty threat mums
- Wait until your father gets home.
- Where's the wooden spoon?

Cranky mums
- Don't use that tone with me!
- Don't you have anything better to do?
- Go to your room and think about what you did!

- Don't hit your sister/brother!
- I don't care who started it, I said stop!
- If I catch you doing that one more time, I'll …
- If I want your opinion I'll ask for it!
- If I've told you once … I've told you a thousand times.

Feeding mums

- If you don't clean your plate, you won't get any dessert.
- You'll sit there until you eat it.
- You just ate an hour ago!
- How do you know you don't like it if you haven't tasted it?
- Eat up all your dinner, think of the starving children in Africa.
- Eat your crusts and you'll get curly hair.
- Eat your carrots and you'll see in the dark.

Avoiding mums

- Ask your father.

Grooming mums

- If you don't wash behind your ears, you'll grow potatoes there.
- Always wear clean underwear in case you get run over by a bus.
- Nice girls don't wear red nail polish on their toes.
- Never talk with your mouth full.
- Don't shave your legs or the hairs will grow back thick and nasty.

Instructive mums
- If a job's worth doing, it's worth doing well.
- If you can't say something nice, don't say anything at all.
- Be happy, but you need to work at your life …
- Don't stay up too late.
- It's as easy to fall in love with a rich man, as a poor man.
- A lady never eats or smokes in the street.
- A lady never whistles.
- A lady always leaves a little bit on her plate.

Annoying mums
- I'll treat you like an adult when you start acting like one.
- Who are you going with? Do I know them?

Vindictive mums
- You made your bed, now lie in it.
- You've only got what you deserve.

Fed-up mums
- Bored! How can you be bored? I was never bored at your age.
- I can give you something to do if you're bored. Tidy your room!
- If you don't stop crying, I am going to give you something to cry about!
- Close the door. Were you born in a tent?
- As long as you live under my roof, you'll do as I say.

- You wait, my girl, your turn will come.
- Beds are NOT made for jumping on.
- Running away? Is that a threat or a promise?
- When did your last slave die?
- What if everyone jumped off a cliff? Would you do it, too?
- I don't care what 'everyone' is doing. I care what YOU are doing!
- You'd forget your head if it wasn't attached to your neck!
- You're going to put your eye out with that thing!
- It will end in tears.
- Are you chewing bricks or just spitting gravel my way?

Warning mums
- Never trust a man in worn down shoes.
- Never trust a man in a brown suit.
- Never trust a man in brown suede shoes.
- Never trust a man whose eyebrows meet.
- Never trust a man with more than two mobile phones.
- Never trust a man who wears a bow tie.
- Never trust a man who is rude to his mother.
- Never trust a man who tucks his jumper into his trousers.
- Men are all right – for chopping wood!
- Never trust a woman who claims to love all sports.
- Never trust a woman who lies about her age.

Picking mums

- Are you going out dressed like that?
- I thought your hair looked lovely the way you had it before.
- Your hair used to be such a pretty colour.
- A little lipstick will add a bit of colour.
- Do you still hear from that nice Bruce/James/Jane/Michelle?
- Do you think the baby's looking a bit thin?
- Do you think your dress is a little tight?
- I used to have a tea towel just like that dress.

Guilt inducing mums

- You make my life a misery!
- I just want what's best for you.
- I will always love you – no matter what.
- I hope someday you have children just like you.
- Call me when you get there, just so I know you're okay.
- I'm not always going to be around to do these things for you.
- When you have kids of your own you'll understand.
- So nice to catch you, I know you're busy.
- I'm useless.
- I was just checking I was ringing the right number.
- You will ALWAYS be my baby.

Rules to live by mums

- Leave someone between you and the sharks.

A MOTHER'S LAMENT

It's an age thing I know —
when I see multiple nose rings
I want to ask,
'Does it hurt when you blow?'

MAUREEN EDWARDS, AUTHOR

WHAT MUMS OF CELEBRITIES SAY

My mother said it was simple to keep a man,
you must be a maid in the living room, a cook
in the kitchen, and a whore in the bedroom.
I said I'd hire the other two and take care of
the bedroom bit.

JERRY HALL, MODEL

❧

'What a pity, Barry. You used to be so nice.'

LOUISA HUMPHRIES TO HER SON, BARRY

❧

Sometimes when I look at all my children, I say to myself, 'Lillian, you should have stayed a virgin.'

LILLIAN CARTER, AT THE 1980 DEMOCRATIC CONVENTION, where her son was nominated for a second term as US president

❧

My mother never saw the irony
in calling me a son-of-a-bitch.

JACK NICHOLSON, ACTOR

❧

CHAPTER 12

Bringing up baby

Parents can read every book,
watch every instructive film, but once the baby
arrives, it's on-the-job training. And the trouble
is just once you think you've worked out
how to do it, baby number two arrives.

JUMPING IN TO CHILD-REARING

Children today are tyrants.

They contradict their parents,

gobble their food,

and tyrannise their teachers.

SOCRATES

❧

Parents who are afraid to put their foot down

usually have children who step on their toes.

CHINESE PROVERB

❧

We spend the first twelve months of our children's
lives teaching them to walk and the next twelve
telling them to sit down and shut up.

PHYLLIS DILLER, COMEDIAN

❧

Like all mothers, we pretend that we don't have favourites but we do. Actually every night before my three kids go to sleep, I whisper into each of their ears: 'You're not my favourite, but you're getting pretty close.' You know, just to keep them on their toes.

CATHERINE DEVENY, AUTHOR/COMEDIAN

Children are like dogs.
They really shouldn't be inside;
they need to run and use their bodies.

RACHEL GRIFFITHS, ACTRESS

The real menace in dealing with a five-year-old
is that in no time at all you
begin to sound like a five-year-old.

JEAN KERR, AUTHOR/HUMORIST

AUSTRALIAN CHILDREN

In Australia a model child is – I say it not without thankfulness – an unknown quantity.

It may be that the miasmas of naughtiness develop best in the sunny brilliance of our atmosphere. It may be that the land and the people are young-hearted together, and the children's spirits not crushed and saddened by the shadow of long years' sorrowful history.

There is a lurking sparkle of joyousness and rebellion and mischief in nature here, and therefore in children.

ETHEL TURNER, *SEVEN LITTLE AUSTRALIANS*

COMPETITIVE MOTHERS

I heard about this madwoman – let's file her under 'every mothers group has one'. When the babies were trying 'tummy time', the mad woman's daughter used to go into a hysterical fit the minute she was put on the mat. On the second week of this happening, the madwoman said: 'Hubby and I are both high achievers, and we think she doesn't like it because she's not good at it.' The baby was nine weeks old.

CATHERINE DEVENY, AUTHOR/COMEDIAN

KEEPING AN EYE TO THE FUTURE

Be nice to your children,
for they will choose your rest home.

PHYLLIS DILLER, COMEDIAN

❧

Children begin by loving their parents;
as they grow older they judge them;
sometimes they forgive them.

OSCAR WILDE, PLAYWRIGHT

STRICT CHILDREN

I am not allowed to
sing, dance, laugh or wear short skirts.
Having a teenage daughter
is like living with the Taliban.

KATHY LETTE, AUTHOR

❧

Mummy herself has told us that she looked upon us more as her friends than as her daughters. Now that is very fine, but still, a friend can't take a mother's place. I need my mother as an example which I can follow.

I want to be able to respect her.

ANNE FRANK, *DIARY OF A YOUNG GIRL*

FRUSTRATIONS

The story of a mother's life:
Trapped between a scream and a hug.

CATHY GUISEWITE, *LIKE MOTHER, LIKE DAUGHTER*

❧

There are only two things a child will share willingly – communicable diseases and his mother's age.

BENJAMIN SPOCK, AUTHOR/CHILDCARE EXPERT

❧

Motherhood is a wonderful thing –
what a pity to waste it on children.

JUDITH PUGH, ART DEALER/WRITER

❧

Parenthood:

That state of being better chaperoned

than you were before marriage.

Marcelene Cox, humorist

WHAT CHILDREN BRING

Wendy Harmer speaks of her children's reaction when they watched her appear on Talking Heads, *ABC, and discuss growing up with a cleft palate.*

It was very interesting that they sat there and they watched the program very thoughtfully, and they didn't say anything too much. I think they were about six and eight at the time, probably. And it was about, say, a month later and Marley said, 'What did happen to you, Mum, when you were born?' And I said, you know, 'I was born without the roof of my mouth,' da da da, and he said, 'Oh, I've heard of that.' He said, 'The doctors fixed you up, Mum, didn't they?' He said, 'Oh, they did a very good job, you're very beautiful.' And Maeve said, 'Yes, Mama, you're the most beautiful woman in the world! Can we get an ice cream?'

And I must confess to driving off to get a slushie with tears pouring down my cheeks. And the whole thing … the whole thing really healed my heart, I think. It really healed me. And so all those years of looking for approbation and looking for love and everything, those two little people just did it for me that afternoon in the back seat of the car. Quite amazing, isn't it? Quite amazing what children bring to you.

CHAPTER 13

Singing the motherhood blues

However much we love our mothers,
most of us get irritated, resentful and ambivalent
towards them at times. And vice versa, even the
most loving mother will feel a twinge of annoyance
at her beloved child. The mother-child relationship
is the one that can never be broken. Our mothers
will love us no matter what happens.

THAT TWISTED FEELING

A Freudian slip is when you say one thing
but mean a mother.

ANONYMOUS

❧

That dear octopus from whose tentacles
we never quite escape, nor in our
innermost hearts never quite wish to.

DODIE SMITH, AUTHOR

❧

My love for her and my hate for her are so bafflingly
intertwined that I can hardly see her. I never know
who is who. She is me and I am she and we're all
together.

ERICA JONG, AUTHOR

BREAKING AWAY FROM MUM

One day, children will leave home and begin lives of their own. This can be hard for both the child and the mother.

❧

The mother-child relationship is paradoxical and, in a sense, tragic. It requires the most intense love on the mother's side, yet this very love must help the child grow away from the mother, and to become fully independent.

ERICH FROMM, SOCIAL PSYCHOLOGIST/AUTHOR

❧

A mother should be like a quilt –
she should keep the children warm
but not smother them.

EC McKENZIE, AUTHOR

❧

It kills you to see them grow up.
But I guess it would kill you quicker
if they didn't.

BARBARA KINGSOLVER, *ANIMAL DREAMS*

But the reason I went [left Australia for England], I think, was that it was a necessary breaking away from a relationship that was too close. I thought the world of my mother and of her generation. They were brave, brave women. But the quickest way for a young man to cripple himself was to stay, I thought. I don't know whether I was right about that or not. I bear a load of guilt about it.

CLIVE JAMES, AUTHOR/CRITIC/POET

❧

The best way to keep children home
is to make the home atmosphere pleasant
and let the air out of the tires.

DOROTHY PARKER, HUMORIST

❧

IT'S A WORRY WHEN CHILDREN DON'T LEAVE HOME

A boy's best friend is his mother.

ANTHONY PERKINS, PSYCHO

❧

RULES FOR VISITING GROWN-UP CHILDREN

- Under no circumstances comment on the state of the bathroom. Any need for comment can be avoided if you take care to use your own facilities before you leave home.

- Never arrive unannounced. Give your child time to shove out the girlfriend/boyfriend, actually any friends as you'll be sure to be embarrassing.

- Do not cast silent glances around the room. It's safest to focus on your child's face so any stray glances are not construed as being judgemental.

- Never, ever do impromptu cleaning unless you are asked. This suggests to your child that you think they can't look after themselves.

- Remind yourself that you don't need to live there, and it's your child's own business if they want to live in a hovel.

- Remember what you do and say will always matter to your children. Be kind to yourself and to your grown child by being uncritical and supportive. The world's already critical and competitive enough.

Don't worry, they'll come back
You see much more of your kids
once they leave home.

LUCILLE BALL, COMEDIAN/ACTRESS

MUMS MAKING HONEST MISTAKES

I stopped believing in Santa Claus when my
mother took me to see him in a department store,
and he asked for my autograph.

SHIRLEY TEMPLE, ACTRESS

MISGUIDED MOTHERS

In his memoir, *My Life as Me*, Barry Humphries tells
how when he was nine he returned home from school
and all his books had disappeared. 'What happened
to my books?' he asked. 'Oh, you've read them,' his
mother said. 'A nice man from the Salvation Army came
and took them away.' For the rest of his life, he says, he
has searched for replicas of these same books.

MOTHERS WHO GOT IT WRONG

Mother always said
that honesty was the best policy,
and money isn't everything.
She was wrong about other things too.

GERALD BARZAN, HUMORIST

DIFFERENT WAYS OF SEEING

My mother and I could always look out the same
window without ever seeing the same thing.

GLORIA SWANSON, ACTRESS

OUCH

I don't think my parents like me.
They put a live teddy bear in my crib.

WOODY ALLEN, ACTOR/DIRECTOR

If God lets me live, I shall attain more than mummy ever has done. I shall not remain insignificant, I shall work in the world and for mankind.

ANNE FRANK, *DIARY OF A YOUNG GIRL*

⁂

[On loving mother] …Yes I did.
As far as it was possible. It wasn't always easy.
She was a very distant person.

BARRY HUMPHRIES, COMEDIAN/AUTHOR/DADAIST

⁂

Don't hold your parents up to contempt.
After all, you are their son, and it is just possible
that you may take after them.

EVELYN WAUGH, AUTHOR

EMBARRASSING MOTHERS

On looking through the washing, Miss Day had exclaimed in horror at the way in which her stockings were mended.

'Whoever did it? They've been done since you left here. I would never have passed such darns.'

Laura crimsoned. 'Those? Oh, an old nurse we've got at home. We've had her for years and years – but her eyesight's going now.'

Miss Day sniffed audibly. 'So I should think. To cobble like that!'

They were Mother's darns, hastily made, late at night, and with all Mother's genial impatience at useful sewing as opposed to beautiful. Laura's intention had been to shield Mother from criticism, as well as to spare Miss Day's feelings. But to have done it so clumsily as this! To have had to wince under Miss Day's scepticism. It was only a wonder the governess had not there and then taxed her with the fib. For who believed in old nurses nowadays? They were a stock property, borrowed on the spur of the moment from reading in *The Family Herald*, from Tennyson's *Lady Clare*. Why on earth had such a far-fetched excuse leapt to her tongue? Why could she not have said, Sarah, the maid-of-all-work? Then Miss Day would have no chance to sniff; and she, Laura, could have believed herself believed, instead of having to fret over her own stupidity. But what she would like to know was, why the mending of the stockings at home should not be Sarah's work? Why must it just be Mother – her mother alone – who made herself so disagreeably conspicuous, and not merely by darning the stockings, but, what was a still greater grievance, by not even darning them well?

HENRY HANDEL RICHARDSON, *THE GETTING OF WISDOM*

IT'S ALL THE MOTHER'S FAULT

He hated his mother, with reason. She was solid hell. A big false lying woman; everything about her was virtuous and untrue. Now I know enough to know that no woman should ever marry a man who hated his mother … Deep in Ernest, due to his mother, going back to the indestructible first memories of childhood, was mistrust and fear of women. Which he suffered from always, and made women suffer; and which shows in his writing.

MARTHA GELLHORN, IN A 1969 LETTER
about her ex-husband Ernest Hemingway to her son Sandy

WHEN MUMS GROW OLD

When our mothers grow old we fantasise we will be able to care for them and be a regular little sunbeam in their lives. Unfortunately, our mothers are still our mothers and all their traits that irritate us remain.

❧

There are days when she [my mother] grumbles so relentlessly that the drone of her voice gets into my bones and drains the joy of our everything. Then it's all I can do not to smother her with a pillow, or tip her out of her wheelchair into the lake and hold her head under with my boot. She is as unaware of my mutinous fury as if she were an empress on a throne. Her children confess these murder fantasies to each other, and double up in silent spasms of relief: without laughter it would all be completely unbearable.

HELEN GARNER, *THE FEEL OF STEEL*

⸙

I only could write because she has Alzheimer's; that's the only way I could write the book, 'cause Mum just loathes what I talk about.

But anyway … but I have to say, because of her Alzheimer's, she's really quite rapt in … she thinks I'm a waitress; and she is rapt – she's so proud of me. So it's all worked out very well.

DENISE SCOTT, COMEDIAN/AUTHOR

HOPEFUL MOTHERS

No matter how old a mother is, she watches her middle-aged children for signs of improvement.

FLORIDA SCOTT-MAXWELL,
PLAYWRIGHT/AUTHOR/PSYCHOLOGIST

❧

The heart of a mother is a deep abyss at the bottom of which you will always find forgiveness.

HONORÉ DE BALZAC, AUTHOR

❧

CHAPTER 14

Mums of a certain age

Some mums have Botox needles,
some mums have plastic surgery and
lots of mums just avoid mirrors. But no matter
how many wrinkles they collect,
they're still our mums.

The woman who tells her age
is either too young to have anything to lose or
too old to have anything to gain.

CHINESE PROVERB

❧

Old age ain't no place for sissies.

BETTE DAVIS, ACTRESS

❧

I refuse to admit that I am more than fifty-two,
even if that does make my sons illegitimate.

NANCY ASTOR, FIRST FEMALE BRITISH MEMBER OF
PARLIAMENT/SOCIETY HOSTESS

❧

The really frightening thing about middle-age
is knowing you'll grow out of it.

DORIS DAY, SINGER/ACTRESS

❧

The time will come when it will disgust you to
look in the mirror.

ROSE KENNEDY, MOTHER OF JOHN F KENNEDY,
ASSASSINATED EX US PRESIDENT

A DAUGHTER'S VIEW
OF COSMETIC SURGERY

She didn't look like my mother any more. I was horrified and I knew I had to be happy. I was wrestling with this dilemma of whether to say, 'Mummy, you look beautiful,' and 'Where is my mother?' It was a huge moment in my life [Catterns was twelve] and I remember saying, 'You look really fabulous,' but in my heart I'd lost my mother.

ANGELA CATTERNS, BROADCASTER

EMBRACING THE WRINKLES

A scarf round the neck is so useful

for women of our age,

isn't it, my darling?

DAME EDNA EVERAGE, Barry Humphries' character
of mega-star Melbourne housewife

❧

I refuse to think of them as chin hairs, I think of them as stray eyebrows.

JANETTE BARBAR, STAND-UP COMIC/WRITER

❧

An archaeologist is the best husband
a woman can have. The older she gets the more
interested he is in her.

AGATHA CHRISTIE, AUTHOR

❧

I think your whole life shows in your face
and you should be proud of that.

LAUREN BACALL, ACTRESS

❧

You're never too old to become younger.

MAE WEST, ACTRESS

❧

CHAPTER 15

Loving
our mothers

*No matter how long a mother has gone,
her child never forgets her. Our mums are who
we yearn for in times of sorrow and sickness.
When I am ill, the only thing I wish to eat is my
mother's twice strained chicken broth.*

CELEBRATING OUR MOTHERS – MOTHER'S DAY

This special day has its origins back in Ancient Greece when an annual spring festival was dedicated to the maternal goddess Rhea. In Britain, the 'mothering Sunday' was the day in earlier times when all the children who were away from their homes often learning a trade or working as servants to earn a living, were allowed to return to their homes. Gradually it became a tradition that on this day the family used to gather for a mid-Lenten feast in which the mother was treated as the special guest. The children visited their mums on this day giving treats of cakes and wildflower bouquets.

Anna Jarvis is recognised as the founder of Mother's Day in the US. Her mother inspired her to create a day to honour all mothers, living and dead, and pay tribute to the contributions made by them. Anna began the tradition by sending carnations (her mother's favourite flower) to her local church, and lobbied the government until the second Sunday in May was designated Mother's Day.

BEST MOTHER'S DAY GIFTS

Many mums would like a ticket to somewhere exotic or exciting, but most of us are happy with a handmade card with a sincere message inside. Here are some suggestions to accompany the card.

- A good bottle of perfume
- A good bottle of wine
- A fancy digital camera
- Some nice photo frames
- Latest book by favourite author
- DVD of favourite television series
- A rose bush
- Gourmet food
- Voucher for spa retreat
- Travel guide book to country where Mum wants to go
- Time with children and a fun family outing
- Breakfast in bed

❧

Breakfast in bed

chocolate milk & toast with sprinkles

Mother's Day

MARY HIND, POET

UNWELCOME MOTHER'S DAY PRESENTS

- *Any kitchen appliance*
  On no planet does a toaster suggest, 'I love you,
  Mum'. Ditto washing machine, blender and iron.
  These are necessities and all create work for mothers.

- *A saucepan set*
  This screams 'Cook me dinner!', and Mother's Day
  is the day that mums expect not to have to worry
  about cooking.

- *Cleaning supplies*
  Even if they're green and wrapped in a fancy bio-
  degradable package to appeal to the eco-conscious
  mother, they should not be presented on Mother's
  Day. Cleaning the house would be a much more
  appreciated gift.

- *A knife set*
  Even the most 'cutting edge' knives should be
  banned as a possible present. They scream 'Cook
  for us!' and for the superstitious, the gift of knives
  severs relationships unless the receiver hands over
  a token amount. But give it a miss on Mother's Day.

- *Anything diet related*
  Self-explanatory.

LOVING OUR MOTHERS

Mother, I love you so.

Said the child, I love you more than I know.

She laid her head on her mother's arm,

And the love between them kept them warm.

STEVIE SMITH, POET

❧

When I stopped seeing my mother

through the eyes of a child.

I saw the woman who helped me

to give birth to myself.

NANCY FRIDAY, *MY MOTHER, MYSELF*

❧

Whatever else is unsure in this stinking

dunghill of a world a mother's love is not.

JAMES JOYCE, AUTHOR

❧

She tried in every way to understand me, and she succeeded. It was this deep, loving understanding as long as she lived that more than anything else helped and sustained me on my way to success.

MAE WEST, ACTRESS

❧

The mother is everything –

she is our consolation in sorrow, our hope

in misery, and our strength in weakness.

She is the source of love, mercy,

sympathy, and forgiveness.

He who loses his mother loses a pure soul

who blesses and guards him constantly.

KAHLIL GIBRAN, POET/ARTIST

REMEMBERING OUR MOTHERS

I miss thee, my Mother! Thy image is still
The deepest impressed on my heart.

ELIZA COOK, AUTHOR

❧

I miss her all the time. Her voice, her smile, her
love, her wisdom. But part of her has merged with
me: You never get over being a child, as long as
you have a mother to go to.

SARAH ORNE JEWETT, AUTHOR

❧

Until I was in the forties … the presence of my mother obsessed me. I could hear her voice, see her, imagine what she would do or say as I went about my day's doings. She was one of the invisible presences who play so important a part in every life.

VIRGINIA WOOLFE, *MOMENTS OF BEING*

One of the godmothers of my gray mood has been a consciousness that on Wednesday the twenty-ninth, it will be a year and a day since my mother died. I miss her a lot. I had new author photos taken and one of them is really gorgeous. I feel sad that she's the only person for whom I would have made a print, framed it and sent it to. Daddy would appreciate it but he couldn't see it. The sense of a safe haven left with my mom because she always wanted to hear about my deepest thoughts and feelings. That's not how my father operates and that's fine, too. I couldn't talk about Sibelius or fifteenth-century England with my mother.

FRANCES KUFFELL, AUTHOR

Acknowledgements

The author would like to thank the following people for their contributions.

Joan Barnes; Nola Bartak; Aleesah Darlison; Catherine Deveny; Maureen Edwards; Anne Gracie; Mary Hind; Frances Kuffell; Judith McLean; Denise Norman; Kay Readdy; Alan, Sarah and Andrew Reynolds; Julia Taylor; Jill Veitch.

Excerpts from the following books appear with thanks:

Margaret Drabble, *The Millstone*, Penguin Books, 2010; George Eliot, *Daniel Deronda*, Oxford University Press, 1998; Nora Ephron, *Heartburn*, Little, Brown Book Group, 2008; *Anne Frank, Diary of a Young Girl*, Penguin Books, 1998; Nancy Friday, *My Mother, My Self*, HarperCollins Publishers, 1994; Helen Garner, *The Spare Room*, Text Publishing Co., 2008; Helen Garner, *The Feel of Steel*, Pan Macmillan Australia, 2001; Kate Grenville, *Joan Makes History*, University of Queensland Press, 2002; Kate Grenville, *Lilian's story*, Canongate Press, 2007; Kate Grenville, *The Idea of Perfection*, Pan Macmillan Pty Ltd, 2000; Cathy Guisewite, *Like Mother, Like Daughter*, Andrews McMeel Publishing, 1993; Barry Humphries, *My Life as Me*, Viking, 2002; Sarah James, *Midwife Wisdom, Mother Love*, Hachette Australia, 2005; Barbara Kingsolver, *Animal Dreams*, Little, Brown Book Group, 1992; Mary McCarthy, *The Group*, Little, Brown Book Group, 2009; Nancy Mitford, *The Pursuit of Love*, Penguin Books Ltd, 2010; Fiona Neill, *The Secret Life of a Slummy Mummy*, Cornerstone, 2008; Ruth Park, *Harp in the South*, Penguin Books Ltd, 2009; Denise Scott, *All That Happened at Number 26*, Hardie Grant Books, 2009; Harriet Walter, *Mothers by Daughters*, ed. Joanna Goldsworthy Virago Press Ltd., 1995